THE BIG RAI$E

THE BIG

PAGE TWO

RAI$E

The Four Stages of Raising Capital for Start-Up Owners and Entrepreneurs

MICHAEL MILLER
ALEXANDER BAKER

Nothing in this document is or purports to be legal or financial advice of any nature or kind and it shall not be relied upon as such under any circumstances for any reason. The authors hereby expressly disclaim any and all responsibility and liability for any reliance at any time by any reader or other party on any of the content in this document or directed to by this document for any legal, financial, investment or other advisory or business purposes, or any other purposes, including any losses resulting therefrom. Any reader, by reading beyond this point, is hereby deemed to have (i) expressly accepted that nothing in this document is presented, designed or conveyed to provide legal, financial, investment or other advice and acknowledged and agreed there shall not under any circumstances be created or deemed to be created an advisor-client or attorney-client relationship or any similar relationship for any reason whatsoever, (ii) expressly disclaimed any reliance on any contents of this document for any legal, financial, investment or other advisory purposes, or any other purposes, and (iii) hereby releases the authors from any and all causes of action, claims and other legal proceedings of any nature or kind relating to this document and its contents.

Cataloguing in publication information is
available from Library and Archives Canada.
ISBN 978-1-77458-324-1 (paperback)
ISBN 978-1-77458-325-8 (ebook)

Page Two
pagetwo.com

Edited by Steve Woodward
Copyedited by Tilman Lewis
Cover and interior design by Jennifer Lum

thebigraise.net

*With great appreciation for the time and effort
of the many entrepreneurs, investment professionals, lawyers,
and accountants who reviewed and commented on
this work throughout its creation.*

Contents

Introduction

INVESTORS NEED many reasons to say yes to invest, but only one to say no.

If you want to get to "yes," keep reading.

Media headlines routinely catalog successful fundraising efforts by savvy entrepreneurs, but rarely mention the thousands who come up empty-handed. We don't blame the press for this. "John fails to win over another investor" is a stale headline. Yet despite the challenges, countless founders throw themselves into the intense, exhausting, and even outright baffling fundraising process, hoping to raise money for their businesses.

Entrepreneurs assume the risks of starting a business for a variety of reasons. They may venture out on their own for a chance to captain their own ship, to earn well beyond their potential as someone else's employee, or to bring a new idea or product to market. Few among us can fund our ideas independently. To realize their vision, entrepreneurs need to source capital (money) for their company from other people and institutions.

Investors who entrust their money with founders require far more than a good idea and a compelling story. Both are essential, but many good ideas have remained unfunded simply because the entrepreneurs weren't properly educated or coached on the nuances and complexity of the fundraising process. Investors placing high-risk bets on emerging companies have their own standards and expectations to be satisfied before they wire funds.

The Big Raise is for you if you want to understand what investors care about, what unforced errors to avoid, and how entrepreneurs can inadvertently make the fundraising process harder than it needs to be. It doesn't matter if you've never raised money before, you have no background in finance, or you've just started tinkering in your garage. This book was written to equip all entrepreneurs with actionable knowledge about raising money to help them compel prospective investors to sign on the dotted line.

The Big Raise is broken into four stages, tracking the journey of an entrepreneur trying to raise money.

Stage one focuses on ideation, when you first develop the idea behind a new technology, product, business model, brand, or way of doing things.

Stage two looks at preparation, when you recognize you need money to realize your vision and begin assembling key materials to present your case to investors.

Stage three addresses the raise itself and what investors need to see and hear to cut a check, which you want to know *before* you pitch.

Stage four reminds you that, if you're fortunate enough to raise money, there are certain things you'll have to do after the money lands if you hope to ever raise money again.

Mistakes are great teachers, but it's better if they're someone else's. To that end, we've included "blown raise stories" about real entrepreneurs who were unsuccessful at raising capital due to a critical error, misconception, or omission that soured investors. (All the names and industries have been changed for privacy reasons.) These stories provide illustrative examples of how *not* to raise money.

We hope this book is good for your sanity, good for a read, and good for helping you achieve your wildest dreams.

Who's Who in Early-Stage and Growth Investing

DURING YOUR fundraising journey, you will encounter many different characters and organizations. Since we will refer to these people and places throughout the book, we want to familiarize you with a few of the most common ones before getting started. If you've been through a raise before or are generally familiar with the players in capital markets (venture capital funds, private equity funds, investment banks, accelerators, incubators, etc.)—including what they do and how they operate—then feel free to jump to chapter one.

People

Founders are individual entrepreneurs, such as Microsoft's Bill Gates or Apple's Steve Jobs, who wander into the corporate wilderness and create their own businesses. Many recognize early on that they will need to work with a larger group of **co-founders** and investors for their business to get off the ground. For many founders, the decision to launch their own company represents their first foray into entrepreneurship, so some elements of running their own business or raising money may be entirely new. At the other end of the spectrum, there are founders with a history of starting multiple businesses, who may describe themselves as **serial entrepreneurs**. Regardless of entrepreneurial experience, every founder will have their own respective strengths, specializations, and weaknesses.

Investors are individuals and organizations willing to put their money at risk to generate financial returns. (In other words, turn their money into more money.) Every investor has varying expectations for risk, returns, and the desired time to realize those returns (i.e., get cash in the bank). Given the relatively high risk and potential complexity of investing in early-stage companies, relatively cautious (and rational) investors will instead opt for more established players like Coca-Cola or McDonald's. Some investors willingly accept the risks associated with investing in nascent companies in exchange for the chance to generate a fantastic return (much more than Coca-Cola or McDonald's can offer). These more risk-tolerant investors can be broken down into several sub-groups.

Angel investors, or simply "**angels**," are individuals who put their own money into companies at the earliest stages, when those companies may be little more than an idea scribbled on paper. Angels are typically wealthy enough to make high-risk bets on potential breakout successes. All angels have their own approaches to investing. Some may invest a few thousand dollars, while others may toss in hundreds of thousands. Some angels mostly sit back and leave you to run the business, while others assume an active role by closely overseeing your operation and providing frequent advice. Angels hail from all backgrounds and have accumulated their wealth from a variety of different means. Some are former founders themselves who have experienced the struggle of building their own businesses (such as PayPal co-founder Peter Thiel, who was an angel investor in Facebook), while others inherited money after their grandparents did the hard part.

On occasion, angel investors organize themselves into an **angel network**. These organizations help angels collaborate on deal opportunities and share resources. Angel networks typically have a niche investment focus (i.e., one might deal within a specific industry, technology, or geographic region). Some angel networks are highly structured, while others are a loose affiliation involving little more than a social media page.

Family offices are firms that manage the finances and investments of a wealthy family, such as Walmart's Walton family, or even just a single high-net-worth individual (think tens of millions or even billions of dollars). While every family office is structured to accommodate the family's unique financial objectives, the common underlying mandate is to protect and grow the wealth. These offices have become increasingly popular over the past several decades as extraordinary increases in wealth, particularly among those in the tech sector, have created a demand for more sophisticated financial planning. Some family offices steer clear of early-stage opportunities, but others are more adventurous and open to participating in a young company's earliest fundraising rounds.

Private equity funds, **PE funds**, or just **PE**, all refer to organizations that invest in private companies, as opposed to public companies whose shares are traded on exchanges like the New York Stock Exchange. These firms are run by specialized fund managers who raise money from a variety of individuals and institutions. The mandate of every PE fund is different, and each may choose to only invest in companies that are engaged in a specific activity, of a certain size, or at a specific phase of their life cycle. Though many PE funds will not even consider investing in a company at its earliest stages, there is an entire class of PE dedicated to doing just that.

Venture capital funds, VC funds, or just **VC**, all refer to a type of private equity fund specializing in funding high-potential emerging companies. Many institutional investors (pension funds, university endowments, etc.) and individuals have recognized that investing some money in emerging opportunities can improve their investment portfolio's overall returns, but they may lack the necessary resources or expertise to intelligently invest in them. Someone may want to get in early on the next Amazon but might not know what qualities to look for or how to find these companies.

Enter VC funds, such as Andreesen Horowitz and the Foundry Group. VC funds are entities that provide a way for individuals and organizations to invest in emerging companies by pooling those parties' money into a single investment fund. Dedicated fund managers then select which companies to invest in. (There are also ways for people who satisfy certain criteria to invest in early-stage companies through online markets—more on that later.)

With so many diverse and emerging high-growth industries, venture capital funds often specialize in, and restrict their investment activity to, one or a handful of industries that align with the fund managers' expertise. For example, some venture capital funds invest in only biotechnology companies, while others invest in only financial technology companies. VC funds frequently play an active role in the oversight of their portfolio companies and connect them with specialized experts, potential recruits and customers, and future investors.

A key difference between angel investors and venture capital funds is that angels are directly investing their own money, while VC funds invest the money of other individuals and institutions on their behalf. (Technically, most VC fund managers are expected to contribute some of their own money into the pool of investable money, but the lion's share of the money

(95%–99%) comes from external investors).[1] These external investors could be pension funds, endowments, governments, high-net-worth individuals, or other organizations that want a piece of the emerging company action.

Strategic investors, or "**strategics**," are organizations that invest with the principal motive of securing a strategic advantage for themselves. While they still seek a financial return on their investment, their primary goal is to secure a strategic interest, such as access to a new technology or service that is being developed. A strategic investor will typically operate in the same or an adjacent industry as their investment target. The frequency with which they make new investments can vary based on the opportunities presented to them, their strategic needs, and their access to and cost of capital.

Many of the largest companies in the world recognize that they have both the capital and technical expertise to consistently vet and support emerging companies and have set up their own **corporate venture capital** divisions. Examples of a few such high-profile divisions include Google's Google Ventures and Salesforce's Salesforce Ventures. These venture divisions can offer companies they invest in many benefits beyond cash, such as access to specialized services, technical assistance, and the means to secure new customers. The companies these divisions invest in can often become acquisition targets of their parent company, which can be very lucrative and convenient for founders but can also close some doors. Every choice involves a trade-off.

Investment banks, like Goldman Sachs, often appear in financial media under headlines highlighting how they successfully help companies raise hundreds of millions, if not billions, of dollars. When people outside the corporate world hear the word "bank," they usually think of institutions that take deposits, facilitate bill payments, and maybe help them with personal financial planning. Those are not investment banks. Rather, investment banks specialize in an array of financial services that companies need. Raising money from external investors is an important one.

So, if you want to raise money, why not go straight to an investment bank? Because investment banks mostly serve companies with proven business models and a history of success (the types of companies listed on stock exchanges or bought by PE funds). Keep in mind that investment banks get the money they raise for these companies from institutions and wealthy individuals, who must be persuaded to invest. These investors generally don't look to investment banks for financial exposure to highly speculative companies, whose limited operating history means their value could literally drop to zero on a moment's notice. For that exposure, these investors will allocate a relatively small chunk of their investment portfolio to a VC fund.

Different types of organizations do different things. Investment banks are more typical for mature companies than those serviced by VC funds. If your new company gains success over the years, then one day you'll likely rub up against investment banks to help service your capital needs. In the early years, though, getting money from them is generally a non-starter.

Places

Co-working spaces, like WeWork, are communal spaces where multiple businesses can operate. They are used frequently by entrepreneurs in the earliest stages. During that time, money is likely tight, the number of desks you need may change from week to week, and the uncertainty of the company's future may make you reluctant to lock in a longer-term lease. Some co-working spaces provide only a physical space, while others offer shared amenities. Some host their own events or provide other resources, such as mentorship opportunities.

Incubators are programs offering entrepreneurs a range of services to help get their ideas off the ground. These programs may be hosted by universities, corporations, governments, or other local institutions. They often provide working space for companies in their program. These programs, which can last from a few weeks to several months, are designed to equip entrepreneurs with the basic skills and knowledge needed to commercialize their idea and grow their business.

Incubators may provide access to mentorship, introductions to financial and legal professionals, investor meet-and-greets, and other resources to help an entrepreneur refine their business plan. Incubators each have their own intake process for admission to each class, but most recognize they are dealing with companies in their earliest phases, so the intake process may not be particularly demanding. Be aware that while some incubators act as non-profits and charge only nominal fees for their office space and services, others are for-profit and may require more substantive payments. They may even require a piece of your company. Some incubators have small pools of money they use to make direct cash investments in particularly promising companies, but these investments are typically quite small (perhaps in the $50,000 range).

Accelerators are like incubators in that they are programs that frequently provide mentorship, business resources, connections, and a working space for emerging companies. A key difference between an incubator and an accelerator is that while an incubator is suited for companies still finding their footing at their earliest stages, accelerators are for companies further along on their journey and positioned for growth. Admittedly, the line between incubators and accelerators can be blurry, and how the line is drawn is decided by the hosting institution. For example, one accelerator may not consider you for their program until you have revenue, while another may be comfortable with a pre-revenue company developing its patent portfolio. Incubators incubate; accelerators accelerate.

Another key difference is that while incubators can be relatively open to companies from a range of different industries and varying degrees of sophistication, accelerators are often more selective. Accelerators receive many applications and may only accept companies operating within a specific industry. Due to intense competition for spots, accelerators may also have more stringent requirements for selecting entrants. Silicon Valley's Y Combinator is one example of a high-profile accelerator with a particularly rigorous application process. Many accelerators are for-profit and invest their own funds in the best companies they work with.

Online marketplaces are relatively new and have sprouted up as part of the crowdfunding revolution. These are platforms (websites) where individuals can invest directly in emerging companies across a variety of industries. Examples of these marketplaces include StartEngine, Republic, Wefunder, SeedInvest, and Netcapital. Combined, these platforms have helped companies raise hundreds of millions of dollars from hundreds of thousands of investors, many of whom may have invested only a few hundred dollars. Online marketplaces have been making a splash in the start-up world, and it would be a mistake to think they're just a fad. Unfortunately, the ability to use these marketplaces may be limited depending on the investor's location. For example, if someone wanted to invest in an American company despite living elsewhere, they may find that local regulations do not allow it.

STAGE ONE

IDEATION

WHEN AN entrepreneur commits to turning their vision into reality, it marks the beginning of a new phase. You wonder how your idea could work as a business, what's needed to get started, how big the opportunity could be, and whether anyone else is already doing it.

Initially, feelings of purpose and thoughts of market domination (perhaps of future riches and status, too) can foster exuberance. It's possible to believe with an idea so grand that the next logical step is to immediately contact investors to see who's willing to pony up.

Prudent entrepreneurs pause and breathe. Time can be your enemy when you have a good idea, as someone else might be working on something similar, but nonetheless it's important to plan your actions and understand your objectives. You must structure your thinking, catalog your thoughts, paper the initial legal relationships, comply with laws, understand your market, and figure out how you'll address questions from others that you may not have considered.

You may appear passionate while pounding the pavement looking for cash, but passion won't amount to much if your zeal causes you to fumble over the basics: setting up and organizing a business, protecting intellectual property, explaining how the business will make money, and understanding your market landscape. And none of this will matter if you are not prepared to relinquish some control.

Let's get started.

1

Understand How You Create Value

LET'S TALK table stakes. As an entrepreneur, whether you're seeking funding or hoping to bootstrap your way to success, you must be able to clearly articulate the answers to five fundamental questions:

- What problem are you solving?
- Who is the problem being solved for?
- Why does the problem need to be solved?
- How does the company solve this problem?
- What alternatives to your solution are available?

If you can't answer these questions, stop doing everything else until you can. These questions frame the commercial foundation for your idea and are important whether you ultimately seek external funding or not, so address them in the ideation phase. We want you to be ready to face investors, and if you aren't ready to address these fundamental questions, you will look silly to any investor with a clue. We don't want that.

An investor pitch is not the time to find your footing. Think about it: investors will get involved with your company only if they expect to make money. They must believe your company will have sufficient sales to generate certain levels of return for them (more on that later). Without clear answers to these questions, how can they possibly start to assess the company's revenue profile? Investors invest in businesses, not products. Having answers to these questions shows you understand that.

These five questions form the basis for establishing your company's value proposition (a fancy way of saying what a company does, how it works, and why it matters to customers). Your value proposition must be front and center for investors, customers, and everyone else who interacts with your company. Plaster it on your website and make it crystal clear in your pitch. Writing your value proposition is not an opportunity to show off how smart and mysterious you are with something enigmatic. You want customers and investors to be able to easily read and understand your value proposition. Keep it simple, keep it clear. For example, when auto manufacturers first wanted consumers to switch over from the horse and buggy to the car in the early 1900s, they would have wanted to communicate that cars don't get sick, they don't get tired and slow down, they have heated interiors, and they can be used for everyday activities. So, they may have described the value proposition as: "The most convenient, reliable, and comfortable transportation available."

Since your only reason for talking to investors is to get their money, make sure you are clear and concise in articulating your unique value proposition so they understand why your company should get their money. What you don't want to do is tell them:

- That you are "still working on" figuring out how to create value. If that is the case, you should have waited until you had answers before booking the meeting!
- How similar your product or service is to your competitors, instead of explaining how it is superior, how it helps different groups of people, or how it is more accessible, and so on.
- How you think your product or service may be unrelated to the target customers' problem(s).

You never want to appear unclear about what you're doing or why, or as if you're not 100 percent confident the market will welcome your product or service. Passion is good, but passion with a rational and coherent story behind it is better. To that end, practice your answers to these fundamental questions over and over to avoid blunders when it's showtime.

What Problem Are You Solving?

Clearly articulating the problem your company solves provides a valuable starting point for investors to understand what your company is about. The investor may or may not be familiar with the problem, so spend some time providing background. Who bears the cost of the problem now, and is that cost borne mostly in the form of time or money? Is the problem obvious to customers or will it require some education? How big is the problem (in dollar terms)? Tell potential investors this stuff to help them see what you see.

Who Is the Problem Being Solved For?

Investors want to understand the nature of your customer market because its characteristics will help determine how valuable your company could be. If your only plausible customers live in an impossibly remote area, miles from any transportation infrastructure, that's material information investors will want to know. There are many different organizations or groups of people companies may try and sell to (i.e., customer segments), so you'll need to be clear about what customer segment you're targeting.

Does your product or service have mass appeal, or is it tailored to the needs of a narrow set of customers (think Post-it notes vs. night-vision goggles)? Will you have customers with slightly different needs and problems that require you to tailor your product to these different customer segments? Alternatively, do your customers, perhaps in different segments with unrelated needs and problems, all use your product without modification? When you can explain who you are solving the problem for, it helps identify the total addressable market for your product or service (that is, the potential sales dollars available if you had 100 percent of the market share).

Why Does the Problem Need to Be Solved?

Investors want this question answered to assess how likely your product or service is to gain traction with your target customer segment(s). People can sell products and services that resolve certain problems, and make money doing so, only if there is sufficient demand. Is that true for your business? How many potential customers have the problem you solve, and how many of those have the money and are willing to pay your price to resolve it? Answering this question fills in your demand curve.

Demand is driven by many factors. Estimating demand is highly speculative, but understanding certain characteristics of the problem you're solving will help gauge an estimate. Ask these questions:

- Is demand being driven by a human need (food, sex, communication, etc.) or a rule or behavioral change in society (plastic bags, dietary restrictions, etc.)?
- Is there demand to have the problem addressed quickly?
- Is the problem critical or a minor inconvenience?
- Do many people or businesses have this problem or only a few?

Ideally, your solution is a product or service that addresses a critical problem that (1) many people or businesses face, (2) is driven by human or competitive needs, and (3) must be addressed quickly. That's a promising environment for value creation and capture. Once you've answered these questions, you will have a good sense of whether there is a compelling reason why your product or service should exist, and whether it could be commercially viable (i.e., sold for more than it costs to produce).

How Does the Company Solve This Problem?

Time to explain how you solve the problem. You must be very clear about this. If you're this far into the pitch, you have convinced investors there is a problem and a reasonably sized customer base the problem needs to be solved for (i.e., someone would be willing to pay for the solution). Now you must explain how your solution helps those potential customers.

This can be very difficult, especially if your product or service is complex or specialized, or if the investor is unfamiliar with the relevant market. Let the investor's questions dictate the discussion's level of detail. Your default approach should remain centered on a degree of simplicity that would allow an investor unfamiliar with your industry to understand.

Investor meetings are often short (and the investor's attention span can be even shorter). This is the time for you to pique interest so the investor carries the meeting longer than planned or becomes interested enough that they review your materials after the meeting and reach out with follow-up questions.

We cannot emphasize this enough: pictures and analogies simplify things. Pictures are incredibly helpful aids for explaining a company's value proposition and how the company will deliver on that proposition. From a potential customer having a problem, deciding to address it, and choosing to patronize your business for your solution to you closing the sale and providing post-purchase customer service, a well-thought-out diagram can clearly convey how your company manages its value chain (that is, how your company is organized to profitably operate). Analogies offer many of the same benefits, mapping your new concept onto something the investor is (hopefully) already familiar with. Buzzwords aside, you need to help investors understand your business quickly and easily. Then they can analyze whether they can add value (contribute to your growth) and whether you are likely to make them money.

What Alternatives to Your Solution Are Available?

It is very difficult to have customers leave a competitor for your product. American entrepreneur Bill Gross believes that, if you want to build something customers will switch for, your company must aim to create a product that is ten times better than its competitor products.[2] Unless you are the only company solving the problem you've identified, you must know who your competitors are and be able describe their products and services. You also need to articulate why your alternative is distinct or costs less, and why that characteristic will translate into market share capture and, eventually, profitability. If you don't know your competitors and you're speaking with an investor who specializes in your industry, you will look unprepared to someone in the subset of people best suited to fund your company. You don't want this and we don't want this—so be prepared. Know your competitors, what they sell, what their pricing is (if you can get it), and how their offerings are different from and similar to yours.

If you give investors these five pieces of information concisely and clearly, then you are building their trust in your ability to operate and grow your company. This is where you want to be. The value of trust between investors and founders/managers cannot be overstated. Tough times will always be just a day away. Take every opportunity to show investors you're serious about using their money to succeed, so you can skate through the tough times together on a foundation of trust. One way to help them trust you is by knowing how your company creates, provides, and captures value, and by being prepared to answer each of the questions outlined above so that they know it, too.

Five Fundamental Questions in Practice: IV Hydration Therapy in Las Vegas

Las Vegas is filled with fantastic amenities. People from all over the world come to party, gamble, attend concerts... and they often drink more than they probably should. The problem these folks face is dealing with debilitating hangovers that prevent them from enjoying the city's offerings. Vegas tourists are often in town for only a brief time and want to maximize every minute there.

The list of traditional hangover treatments is extensive—drink lots of water, sleep it off, take over-the-counter pain relievers. Regardless of the chosen method, a common thread is that these methods require considerable time for full effect. Sleeping it off may be effective, but it will cost half a day or more of the vacation.

Recognizing the problem, the potential demand from consumers, and the weaknesses of the current solutions, several Las Vegas entrepreneurs launched intravenous (IV) hydration therapy businesses. These operators offer hungover patrons a custom IV drip providing rehydration and specific vitamins and minerals that assist with a relatively rapid recovery.

These businesses garnered success in recent years and can now be found in many of the world's largest cities. Many big cities are full of people who may not have time for a hangover. Regardless of where you find these businesses, any of their founders would be able to clearly articulate to you why they are fulfilling an important need:

- **What problem are you solving?** Being hungover wastes people's time.
- **Who is the problem being solved for?** People living in or visiting dense population centers who had too much to drink and want or need a quick recovery.

- **Why does the problem need to be solved?** Hangovers are frequently occurring physical conditions that will continue to plague many who would prefer they pass more quickly so they can take full advantage of their day.
- **How does the company solve this problem?** By providing ready urban access in select geographic spaces to services designed to efficiently combat the physical symptoms that cause hangovers resulting from alcohol consumption.
- **What alternatives to your solution are available?** Eat, sleep, drink liquids, or take over-the-counter meds or at-home hangover solutions, all of which either take too much time, are inaccessible, or are not particularly effective.

Why does the problem need to be solved? Hair dryers are frequently [illegible] that will continue [illegible] who would [illegible] they [illegible] quickly [illegible]

How does the company solve the problem? By designing [illegible]

[illegible]

2

Consider Your Legal Structure and Obligations

IT IS amazing how fast you can get into trouble in life if you don't know what you are doing. This is particularly true when raising money. We absolutely don't want that for you, so in this chapter we provide some background on protecting yourself from liability.

Setting up a new business without the right knowledge is one way a well-meaning entrepreneur can make things ugly really quickly. Starting a business involves more than racing off to set up a website, get a tax number, and apply for a business license. You must also organize the business with the appropriate legal structure, so you can protect yourself and demonstrate to investors that you act with prudent intention.

The Basics of Limited Liability

Perhaps one of the most important concepts that helped spur investment and economic growth over the last few centuries is "limited liability." In the corporate context, that means the losses a company's equity holders can suffer are limited to the amount of money they invested. If you invest $1,000 into a business whose legal entity structure provides limited liability, then the most you can lose as a shareholder is $1,000. It doesn't matter if the legal entity that operates the business is drowning in debt, can't pay its bills, or is sued into oblivion; as an equity holder, you are not on the hook for any of those debts.

You can imagine how an investment opportunity that fails to provide investors with limited liability is a frightening prospect. If the investors bought a piece of a company that racks up a pile of debt and fails, they could potentially lose their house! Not many would ever invest with this much risk. More importantly, why would an entrepreneur ever choose to organize their business in a way that did not provide themselves, also an owner, with limited liability? Well, it depends on what you are trying to achieve.

Sole Proprietor

The most basic legal structure a business can operate as is a sole proprietorship. Under a sole proprietorship, the owner and the business are one and the same. Your business's assets are your assets, your business's liabilities are your liabilities, and your business's income is your income. Setting these up can be as simple as renting a space and selling T-shirts.

The cost of setting up a sole proprietorship is nominal, and the administrative overhead is lower than other formal legal entity structures, but the owner/operator does not have limited liability. If the company gets into trouble with debts it can't pay, then parties who have been stiffed can come after you and your personal assets. So, if while you're selling shirts you fall behind on your storefront rent, that's your personal problem. There is no liability shield protecting you.

A sole proprietorship is often preferable when a small business is engaged in a relatively low-risk activity not requiring much overhead or any external investors—think tutoring piano. If you're doing anything where real liabilities could accrue or investors' money will be required to grow the business, a sole proprietorship isn't for you. In other words, probably no one reading this book will want to use a sole proprietorship for their venture.

Partnerships

Another legal entity structure used to house an operating business is a general partnership. This structure is often relied on when a few current or would-be sole proprietors decide to join forces in a common pursuit of making money—such as two guys writing a book. A general partnership is like the sole proprietorship in that the partners who operate the business do not have limited liability as owners, and anyone the business is indebted to can go after the partners personally. Once again, this is not ideal if you want your business to really take off.

An alternative to a general partnership, which offers a degree of limited liability for investors, is a limited partnership. In a limited partnership, investors who contribute cash in exchange for a share of the profits, but do not operate the business, are known as the limited partners (LPs). As the name suggests, they have limited liability. (By the way, venture capital funds frequently use this structure. More on that later.) Unfortunately for any general partners (GPs), whether an individual or entity, who may have contributed their own cash and resources and run the business, they do not have limited liability in their capacity as a GP.

So, if as an owner who wants to run their own business, you can't get limited liability for yourself with a sole proprietorship, a general partnership, or even a limited partnership entity structure, what should you do?

Corporations and LLCs

Practically all the world's largest businesses are legally organized as corporations. Corporations are a distinct legal entity that, in countries like the United States and Canada, clearly separates the business's assets from its owners and provides limited liability. The owners of a corporation's equity are referred to as shareholders or stockholders, depending on which jurisdiction the corporation was formed in. They do not own a corporation's assets or hold direct liability for its debts and other obligations. Rather, they own shares or stock in the corporation that owns the assets and is liable for its debts and other obligations. This might seem circular, but this clear legal distinction limits the amount an owner can lose to the amount of money that shareholder invested to purchase the corporation's shares or stock.

If a corporation spirals into debt, its creditors can only chase after the corporation's assets, not the equity owners' personal assets. This practice of governments limiting liability, while providing for the existence and use of corporations for individuals to pool their money in pursuit of economic aims, has made it far easier for entrepreneurs to raise money for new ventures. This concept fundamentally altered the form of cooperative economic work. It's an essential component of the incredible comfort of the modern life many of us enjoy.

Lest you think corporations are wholly superior in every way, there are indeed drawbacks. Corporations have higher administrative costs (including initial incorporation costs), annual filing obligations, and more extensive legal management. Corporations are also taxed as separate legal entities. This means the corporation pays taxes on its profits. Shareholders also pay taxes when those after-tax profits are paid out to them, whether in the form of dividends or as capital gains when the business is sold. Hence, you might hear business types grumble that corporations are subject to "double taxation." Corporations also have extensive governance requirements to ensure shareholders' money and interests are respected. (More on that shortly.)

We would be remiss if we did not offer a clear warning about using a corporation structure for your business: just because a corporation's debts are its own and you have limited liability as an equity holder does *not* mean that you are free of all liability in *all* cases.

If you do something nefarious, grossly negligent, or outright criminal while running your business, it is possible you may be held personally liable in certain limited circumstances (lawyers call this "piercing the corporate veil"). Additionally, if your corporation needed you to personally guarantee a loan it could not otherwise get on its own, and you sign that guarantee, then the company's creditors can still come after you. "Limited liability" is not a Get Out of Jail Free card permitting you to do anything you please without consequence. It's there to protect equity holders, not enable the commission of fraud or criminal actions.

Limited liability companies (LLCs) are another type of legal entity. They are increasingly popular among business owners in the United States (sorry, Canada, your legislatures aren't keeping up). Like corporations, LLCs provide owners with limited liability, but with the bonus of extreme flexibility around their tax status; terms relating to ownership, governance, profit distribution waterfalls; and other matters that can and do fill textbooks. This enhanced flexibility around governance is the big difference between LLCs and corporations.

There are other minor, but important, language differences between corporations and LLCs, too. For example, a corporation's equity holders are shareholders or stockholders, while

LLCs' equity holders are usually members or unitholders. Corporations have directors, but LLCs often have managers (though they can have directors, too; as we said, they're very flexible entities). The key takeaway is that both corporations and LLCs provide limited liability for owners and can be efficient entities to use for organizing and operating your business if you intend to raise third-party capital. If you're reading this book, it's likely you will want to set up your business as an LLC or a corporation.

Governance

When operating as a sole proprietorship, you are free to run your business as you please. How you spend money, what business activities you undertake, and how much you pay yourself are all up to you alone. When your business is a corporation that you do not own 100 percent of, everything changes.

Laws allowing the creation and use of corporations contain extensive rules regarding how they must be run, including who makes decisions and who operates the business from day to day. As a founder, you don't need an intricate understanding of these components—that's what your corporate lawyer is for. But as someone raising capital, you need to understand the basic relationship between three key groups common to corporations around the world: shareholders (or stockholders), directors, and officers.

Shareholders own the business. They may be individuals or entities, such as another corporation, an LLC, or a limited partnership. Some shareholders will work for the company full-time, but most others may have their own jobs or obligations, and therefore won't be overseeing the day-to-day operations. Others may be professional investors (such as venture capital funds). Shareholders want to ensure the corporation is run to serve their interests, which is where their right to appoint directors comes in.

A corporation's **directors** are responsible for managing the business of the corporation on behalf of the shareholders, and they have fiduciary duties (or really serious obligations) to the corporation and its shareholders. Directors are elected by the shareholders, and are collectively referred to as the board of directors or, simply, the board. The number of directors at a company varies; larger companies generally have more directors (eight to twelve) whereas young start-ups may have one to three. The board acts either by a vote of the majority at a board meeting or by a written resolution signed by all the directors.

When raising money from angels and VC funds, it is common for the investors contributing the largest checks to negotiate for one or more board seats (that is, the right to appoint one or more directors). They want a board seat not just for informational and oversight purposes, but to have a vote on major business decisions, including raising money, making acquisitions of material assets or other companies, and appointing those who operate the business, namely, the officers.

A corporation's **officers** are the top-level executives responsible for running the day-to-day business. They are appointed (and can be fired) by the board. Unless a director is also serving as an officer, directors are effectively part-time in their oversight role. Many of them might concurrently serve as a director of other companies. This can be a boon because such directors make more contacts and learn other things that may benefit your business. It can also be a drag because a director may lose focus and be overburdened. Regardless, the officers are responsible for the company's critical business functions.

A corporation's chief executive officer (CEO) is often the most publicly known person at a company (and is usually also a director). CEOs often appear in financial news media or at industry conferences to tout their company's vision, and they bear most of the day-to-day responsibility for forming and executing the strategy of the corporation's business. When you first start your business, you will be the de facto CEO. As your business grows, you will likely need to bring in specialized officers, such as a chief marketing officer or chief legal officer, to manage specific aspects of the business.

The point is: if your business is organized in a corporation, when you take an investor's money in exchange for issuing them shares, you are not going to be left unchecked to run your business solely as you desire. There will be real oversight, requirements to report results, and a need for officers and the board to promote and defend decisions they believe are in the best interests of the business.

Applicable Laws

There can be massive consequences for not taking appropriate steps to abide by the laws applicable to your business, such as environmental or data security and privacy laws. In season four of HBO's *Silicon Valley*, for example, the character Dinesh becomes the CEO of PiperChat. Dinesh is thrilled, and because the platform is experiencing tremendous growth, he lets his newfound power and prestige flow to his head.

Eleven days into his tenure, he learns the company's organic growth is built upon underaged children using the platform. Dinesh hadn't bothered to implement any terms of use or other legal disclaimers relevant to the service. He didn't think it was a big deal, because he hadn't heard of the U.S. Children's Online Privacy Protection Act (COPPA).

Relationship between Directors, Officers, and Shareholders

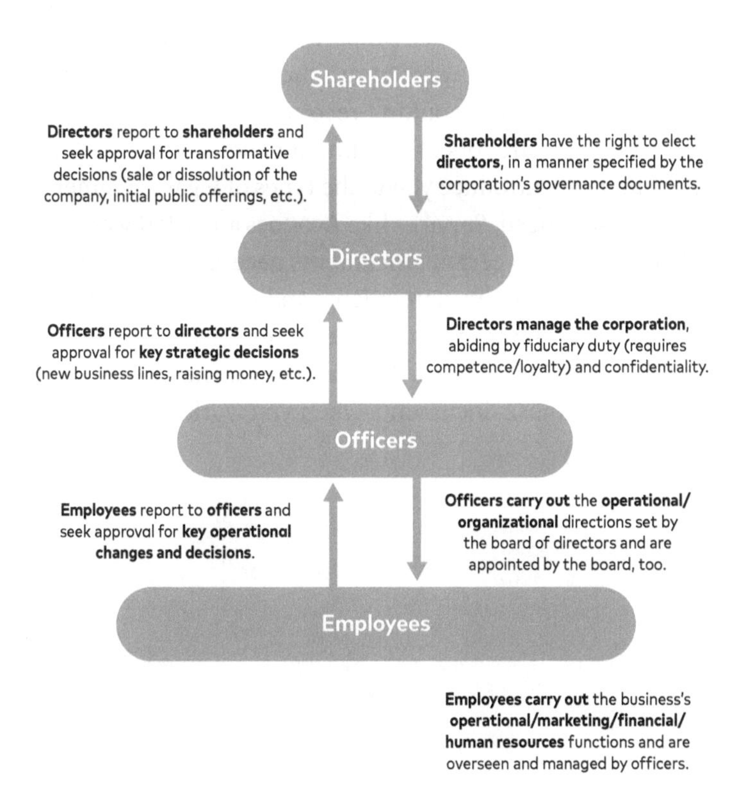

Shareholders
Directors report to shareholders and seek approval for transformative decisions (sale or dissolution of the company, initial public offerings, etc.).
Shareholders have the right to elect directors, in a manner specified by the corporation's governance documents.
Directors
Officers report to directors and seek approval for key strategic decisions (new business lines, raising money, etc.).
Directors manage the corporation, abiding by fiduciary duty (requires competence/loyalty) and confidentiality.
Officers
Employees report to officers and seek approval for key operational changes and decisions.
Officers carry out the operational/organizational directions set by the board of directors and are appointed by the board, too.
Employees
Employees carry out the business's operational/marketing/financial/human resources functions and are overseen and managed by officers.

Unfortunately, the failure to be compliant with the law meant every message sent by every user under the minimum age was a COPPA violation. Based on 51,000 estimated underaged users, *multiplied by* an average 25.6 chat sessions per user, *multiplied by* $16,000 (the penalty per violation), this resulted in approximately $21 billion in fines. While this situation is fictional, something equally scary could very easily become reality for a founder who doesn't take the time to identify, understand, and comply with the laws applicable to their business.

Almost everything your company does will have a legal element to it. It's more than just forming the entity. Many documents will need to be prepared and signed even in the early stages (lest you want to run the risk of ending up like Dinesh). Though we wouldn't recommend relying on these outright, there are lots of document generator services out there that can introduce you to the types of legal agreements that start-ups need. Services like Avodocs and Clerky provide efficient access to certain documents necessary for start-ups, such as confidentiality agreements and more! The resources are out there, so make sure you're taking advantage of them and familiarizing yourself. This may lower the ultimate cost of finalizing these documents when you work on them with your attorney.

3

Prepare to Relinquish Some Ownership and Control

STARTING A new company can be exciting for everyone involved, especially when the founders are first introducing new ideas, new services, or new technologies to the market. Founders are in a unique position because the risks are considerable (no income or job stability and the possibility of wasted time), but the rewards can be spectacular (Silicon Valley–level wealth). Plenty of companies begin in an actual garage or basement and go on to be worth hundreds of millions or billions, enriching their founders and others along the way.

For these companies to successfully navigate their journey, almost all of them needed to win over investors and raise capital. (We say "almost" because there are rare exceptions like Mailchimp, which was able to self-fund and was sold for approximately $12 billion in 2021.) The most common way companies raise money is by selling a piece of ownership to an investor in exchange for cash, specialized services, or property the company requires. This ownership of the company is referred to by many semi-interchangeable terms you may have heard before—equity, shares, stock—and the effect of selling an ownership stake is that certain rights are divided among more owners.

The percentage of a company's equity a new owner receives is based on the ratio between the amount of money they invest (or the value of property or services they provide) and the valuation of the company at the time of the investment. Therefore, when companies look to raise capital by issuing equity, they need to set a valuation.

For example, if a company wants to raise $1 million, it may set a pre-money valuation of $4 million. If that company is successful in raising the $1 million, the company would be said to have a post-money valuation of $5 million and the new investors will own 20 percent of the company. It is very important to understand the difference between pre-money valuation, which is the value before funding has come in, and post-money valuation, which is the value after funding has come in. If you have an entire conversation with an investor about values, but she's talking about post-money and you're talking about pre-money, you will have very different perspectives on post-raise ownership interests.

Investors buy equity because it gives them the right to share in the company's profits and to influence or control certain company decisions. It also gives investors the opportunity, assuming things go well, to eventually sell their ownership at a much higher price than they paid for it, given the company's increased valuation. (Any growth in value beyond the investment price is a "capital gain.") Investors who buy equity in early-stage companies do so understanding it is a high-risk / high-reward opportunity.

Companies may take off and generate fantastic returns for investors who would struggle to replicate this success with later-stage companies. Or companies may collapse, sending the value of the purchased equity to zero. This is the more likely outcome because most start-ups eventually go out of business. According to Tom Eisenmann, a Harvard Business School professor writing about start-ups in the *Harvard Business Review*, "more than two-thirds of them never deliver a positive return."[3]

Understanding Dilution

When you first start a company, you (and your co-founders, if any) will issue equity to yourselves and own 100 percent of the company's equity. As your company sells new equity to investors, your relative ownership will decline (i.e., your ownership is "diluted") to less than 100 percent. Unless you are wealthy enough to fund your new venture on your own and possess the expertise to grow your business without co-founders, dilution is an inevitability you'll have to manage. Investors do not hand out free money; dilution is the price of growth capital.

Unfortunately, entrepreneurs often bristle at the thought of any dilution. They may believe that because it is their company, their idea, and their vision, they should not have to share much of the success. They may also worry that, in the long run, they will lack absolute control of the business and be forced to share decision-making authority with people who may not share their vision for the company. As a counterpoint to this view, consider that through the course of growing Amazon, Jeff Bezos's ownership stake was ultimately diluted to just under 10 percent in 2022—and we're sure he's very happy with his share.

You may be wondering why, if an entrepreneur does not want to give up their company's equity, they don't just borrow the money to avoid selling shares and lowering their ownership percentage. Let's look at that scenario next.

The Problem with Early-Stage Debt Financing

Compared to equity, debt is a lower-reward and lower-risk way to invest in companies. Unlike equity owners who share in undefined profits, lenders define their returns by contractually set interest rates based on the risk profile of the borrower (like a mortgage). When someone with a stable income and a long history of paying back debts borrows money, lenders give them lower interest rates compared to someone who has just taken out their ninth credit card to refinance their eighth. The same is true for companies—those with long operating histories and tangible assets to serve as collateral are more attractive to lenders than start-ups with few physical assets.

All other things being equal, debt is lower risk than equity. This is because if a company falls apart, lenders have contractual rights that ensure they are paid before the shareholders receive whatever is left when the business or its assets are sold. Lending money to young companies is challenging because if the company fails, the lender likely will not recover anything—what is known as getting "zero cents on the dollar." Therefore, the high interest a lender would need to charge to offset the enormous risk would probably blow up the economics of a fledgling company, as it tries to launch new services and focus on growth but isn't yet generating positive cash flow.

Early-stage companies that manage to secure debt financing and avoid equity dilution typically have either (1) a founder wealthy enough to personally guarantee the amount, or (2) a specific company asset that the lender can take if the company defaults. Suffice it to say, most lenders will not accept lines of code for a new app as security.

Lenders look for tangible assets as collateral, which start-ups don't often have, as intellectual property and people are usually the value drivers. Can you imagine getting a mortgage without a house to secure repayment? Neither can we.

If a start-up manages to raise unsecured debt without making any personal guarantees, odds are a favorable government program was involved. In a nutshell, the relative risk of financing a nascent company absent a corresponding upside, and the usual lack of collateral, makes conventional debt financing a practical non-starter for most start-ups. There are a few exceptions.

One of the most prominent exceptions is convertible debt, which generally allows the lender to convert their loan into equity after a set amount of time or when a certain company event has occurred. The amount of equity a convertible debt lender receives in exchange for the amount owed is based on a conversion formula.

For example, a convertible loan may convert into shares of your company at a defined rate of $0.20 per share. In this scenario and assuming a loan balance of $1 million, conversion would leave the lender with 5 million shares of your company. If you had 20 million shares outstanding prior to this conversion, your former lender and newest shareholder would now own 20 percent of the company's equity (5 million divided by total shares outstanding of 25 million).

Convertible debt lenders still charge interest like a more conventional loan, but given how cash-strapped young companies can be, this interest is typically added to the principal amount throughout the life of the loan instead of being paid out regularly in cash. This means that when conversion occurs, the lender receives more equity to account for the accrued interest that has not been paid in cash. Many investors are fond of using convertible debt because they have some downside protection while the loan is outstanding in case your company blows up, but if things go well, they can also convert into equity and share in the longer-term success of the business. The venture capital world has evolved to rely on other securities as well, such as simple agreements for future equity (or SAFE notes). These securities share some features with convertible debt, but often don't charge interest and are not normally convertible at the option of the holder. We'll talk more about these later.

There are other forms of venture lending provided by institutions whereby lenders will make loans to start-ups, but the criteria for securing these loans can include, among other things, a previously successful equity raise from a sufficiently credible external investor of a minimum amount.

Dilution Is Not a Dirty Word

Try to avoid the tendency to think of "dilution" as a dirty word. As we mentioned above, the notion of selling a stake in one's company can be distressing, to the point that some entrepreneurs inadvertently self-sabotage when trying to raise money. This self-sabotage can manifest in several ways, such as approaching investors with a ridiculously high pre-money valuation, or simply refusing to give equity to the co-founders and early employees who investors know will be necessary to the company's success.

If you are looking to raise money for a new venture, you must acknowledge two points. First, with every new round of equity or convertible debt issued, your overall ownership percentage will fall—you will be diluted—and that is not necessarily a bad thing. The money raised is going to help you develop your product or service, hire new people, and sign up more customers. That money will help transform an idea with potential into a tangible business with real value over time.

Second, you should prioritize the absolute value of your shares over your relative piece of the pie. If you continue to win over customers, spend strategically, and raise money at higher valuations, the implied value of your shares will go up.

It is far better to own 20 percent of a company worth $100 million than 100 percent of a company worth $1 million.

Ultimately, if you obsess over maintaining a certain ownership percentage rather than raising money at valuations that will enable you to continue growing your business, you will find yourself in a perpetual struggle to raise capital. We don't want that for you. Of course, you want to minimize dilution, but not to the extent that it impedes your ability to grow. You must be reasonable and temper these two competing interests. You may wonder what level of dilution is acceptable for each round. We'll address that later when we talk about the differences between funding rounds.

Case Study: Capital Stack

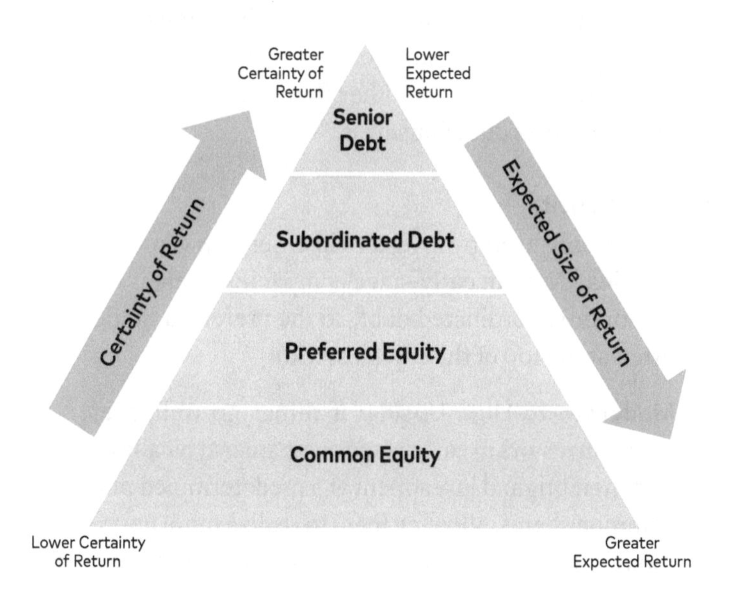

Basic Capital Stack (of a mature company)

Senior Debt

- Commonly referred to as being at the "top of the capital stack."
- **Lowest Upside:** Returns are set by contract and do not include the right to capital gains or dividends, which can be extremely lucrative if the company is successful.
- **Lowest Downside:** They sit on top and will be paid out before anyone else if the company goes out of business.

Subordinated Debt

- **Moderate-to-Low Upside:** Like senior debt, returns are set by contract and do not include the right to capital gains or dividends, but the interest rate subordinated debt is paid will be higher than that received by senior debt.
- **Moderate-to-Low Downside:** They sit on top of all other pieces of the capital stack except senior debt and will be paid out before anyone other than the senior debt if the company goes out of business.

Preferred Equity

- Commonly used by investors in emerging venture opportunities. (*Note:* In early-stage companies, there is often no senior or subordinated debt, so the preferred holders are often at the top of the capital stack.)
- **Moderate-to-High Upside:** If things go well, preferred equity investors in early-stage companies typically can convert their original investment at a predetermined price into common shares, allowing them to realize more upside. The moderate return is realized in the downside case where the company falters but the preferred equity investors recover some money given their priority over common equity.

- **Moderate-to-High Downside:** Often provides investors with special rights and protections, such as the right to have their original investment returned before common equity receives any returns, but preferred holders' returns are still subordinated to debt holders' returns. That means, if the company goes out of business and the liquidation value of the assets is only enough to cover the senior debt and part of the subordinated debt, the pref holders get nothing.

Common Equity

- Commonly referred to as being at the "bottom of the capital stack."
- Commonly owned by founders and those receiving incentive equity.
- **Highest Upside:** Will capture capital gains and dividends if the company is successful. Meaning, they get all the returns after the fixed returns of the other pieces of the capital stack are satisfied.
- **Highest Downside:** No contractual right to a return or priority payment above any other class of equity (i.e., preferred equity) or debt holder, so they are the most likely to lose everything if things go wrong.

4

Don't Tell Just Anyone Your Great New Idea

HAVE YOU developed a fantastic new technology? Can it potentially solve problems while making you millions? Were you so excited that right away you told everyone how it works in detail? Oh dear...

It is totally understandable that your first instinct when having a eureka moment is to tell people about your idea. After all, you may have had an idea no one else on the planet has thought of that could form the basis for a great product or service. No doubt that's something you want to share with others. However, if you tell everyone, it may not be "your" idea much longer.

The Basics of Intellectual Property

Intellectual property, often referred to as just IP, are creations of the mind that include inventions, designs, brands, and creative works of art and literature. Many of the most successful companies in the world rely on the strength and commercialization of their intellectual property to generate extraordinary profits. Whether those intellectual properties are creative works, like Disney's enormous cast of characters (from Mickey Mouse to Ariel); inventions, like the unique technologies contained within Apple's products; or even just a brand like Rolex, signaling high-end value, they all enhance a company's financial results and therefore its value.

Developing and commercializing intellectual property can equip companies with a competitive advantage over their peers, but only if that intellectual property is protected. If your competitors can duplicate your new technology or swipe your original art without the cost and burden of creating it (or paying you), then you are merely equipping them to better compete and eroding any potential competitive advantage.

To prevent others from exploiting the fruits of its innovative labor, a company may pursue formal legal protections to inhibit its competitors from using its intellectual property. These legal protections come in a few forms. Here are some of the most common:

- **Copyright** protects creative works and includes paintings, musical compositions, books, poems, movies, computer programs, and more. In Canada and the United States, once a creator "fixes" their work, by snapping a photograph, recording a song, or writing a book, the creator is automatically a copyright owner. This means they have various rights, including the right to reproduce their creative work and produce derivative works based upon that original work. Companies frequently hire artists for specific projects and will often structure their contracts so that the company itself will be the ultimate owners of the works that are produced. For example, Disney might hire you to write a new Star Wars film script, but your writing, and any new characters or planets you create for your story, would be fully owned by them (because Disney has competent lawyers). It is common for creators to register their work with their country's copyright office, as it allows others to identify the owners of a work and can be required for a creator to take legal action against someone who may have misappropriated their work.

- **Trademarks** are a combination of letters, words, sounds, or symbols that distinguish a company's goods or services from others in the marketplace. You are already familiar with several iconic trademarks, like McDonald's Golden Arches logo and Nike's "Swoosh." Companies that formally register their trademarks with the patent and trademark office enjoy a greater degree of protection compared to those who opt not to register them. Registering trademarks is standard practice for the world's top companies, because the creation of a trademark does not automatically create trademark rights. This is different from copyrights, where creation of the work results in automatic creation of a copyright.

- **Patents** are legal monopolies granted to an inventor by a government allowing the inventor to pursue legal action to exclude others from making, manufacturing, using, and selling the invention for a defined period. In the United States and Canada, this period can span up to twenty years. The purpose of granting this temporary monopoly is to incentivize inventors with a window when only they can profit from their invention. (We'd be remiss if we didn't point out that companies do steal and use other companies' patented technologies without license, but if you own the patent, you have the right to go after these companies legally. You could pursue monetary damages and court orders preventing those other companies from continuing that theft and use.) Examples of iconic inventions that were patented include the lightbulb, perforated toilet paper, and the design of the iPhone. A patent is a form of registered intellectual property; it is not granted automatically upon creation of an invention. The application and examination process for registration is long and complicated.

Patent Protection

Given how many new companies are founded to develop and commercialize a new technology, understanding the basics of how a patent is granted, and how things can go terribly wrong if the patent application process is botched, deserves a deeper dive.

To be granted a patent, an inventor or a company must file a patent application with a patent office. The application discloses all the details of the invention, and includes patent claims that not only define the monopoly they are seeking but also differentiate against prior disclosures. The patent application will eventually be made public by the patent office. The application will be scrutinized by the patent office to ensure it passes the criteria for being granted a patent, which includes, among other things, a need for the invention to be "novel" (i.e., new), non-obvious, and useful.

For an invention to be novel, there must be no prior art or public use or sale of the invention that discloses its differentiated elements. For an invention to be non-obvious, the claimed invention must involve an inventive step over the prior art. For an invention to be useful, it must be functional and operative. Prior art includes existing patent publications, research papers, blog posts, YouTube videos, or any other form of public disclosure. Some patent filings based on existing prior art manage to slip through the patent office and end up as issued patents. If that happens, there is a risk this prior art will be discovered later and the patent retroactively invalidated. Should you successfully navigate this multi-year application and examination process and the patent office determines your invention is novel, non-obvious, and useful, and you pay your grant fee, your patent will be considered "granted."

First-to-File

With so many entrepreneurs, engineers, and inventors around the world, it should not surprise you that, on occasion, more than one person derives an idea for a new technology around the same time. So how is it determined who should own the right to commercialize and exclude others from using these new technologies?

In the United States and Canada, this is determined by the concept of "first-to-file." First-to-file is a legal concept that, in the context of intellectual property law, means whoever files their patent application first will be given priority over those who file later. Filing first does not necessarily mean you will "win" or that your patent will be granted, but it does save your spot in line for a chance to win (i.e., to be the person granted the patent if the filing is successful).

In some countries, including the United States and Canada, if an inventor discloses their invention to the public, they are given a one-year grace period to file their patent application without having their earlier public disclosure impacting their filing date. However, many countries have no grace period, and disclosing your invention before filing can compromise your ability to protect your invention.

Most countries follow a first-to-file system for patents. The United States was the last major holdout before it switched over to this system in 2013. Moreover, many countries are members of the Patent Cooperation Treaty, which facilitates global filing of a patent application with the filing date recognized in 157 different member states as of the date this book was published. Given the global system and the pace of innovation, working with intellectual property professionals to expeditiously file for protection can be critical to your success.

The Slow Burn

Like a lot of other bad decisions in life, the real consequences of not protecting your intellectual property can manifest with a slow burn. It could be years before someone decides your technology is worth copying. It could be years later before you realize your earlier public disclosures and failure to file in time may have invalidated your ability to enforce your patent.

Investors with a sophisticated background in intellectual property will likely ask about your public disclosures. This is especially true if the technology you developed is the linchpin of your future success. Suffice it to say, if you made details of your technology public, investors will want to know how much information you revealed and when. Plenty of deals have blown up simply because of poor early disclosure practices.

As a parting note: this chapter has given you a very light briefing on some of the fundamental concepts of intellectual property. Please understand, this is a complex area of law with an incredible amount of nuance. Our aim is to introduce a variety of concepts to instill a base level of knowledge. If you want to learn more about intellectual property, there are many great resources you can consult. Check out our resource page for more, and if you're devising a new invention, seek professional advice.

Blown Raise Story: A Tale of Two Sisters

Two sisters, one of whom was an engineer and the other a designer, developed plans for an exciting piece of wearable medtech. They used their savings to design and build a crude working prototype.

They initially decided to raise money through a crowdfunding platform to finance finishing the product and getting it market ready. To show off to their potential investors how revolutionary it was, they excitedly uploaded intimate details of their product, including design diagrams, hardware schematics, and other fundamentals about the technology to the crowdfunding platform. The sisters managed to raise a modest amount of money through the platform, and just over a year later, they were ready to approach major investors to finance production.

One of the first questions the two were routinely asked as they went from investor to investor was about their patent filings and what components of the product were protected. When they informed investors that they had not filed for any patents yet, the follow-up question was about their previous disclosures. When it became apparent that the crowdfunding platform had revealed so much intimate information and that it took place more than a year ago, the potential investors concluded that the company would not be able to protect its core technology and they promptly walked away from the deal.

5

Understand Your Environment

YOU'VE DECIDED to solve a problem. Fantastic! Who else is solving it, how are they doing it, and what do you estimate their profit margins are? You don't know? Then it's time to find out. We want you to put your best foot forward, so be prepared. Most investors will ask for this information, and it's best to investigate it while you're still crystallizing your business plan and still in the ideation phase.

Investors expect you to explain the market you're entering and how you fit into it. Simply spouting the trite ambition that your solution will "win over at least 1 percent of the population" will only create concern that you haven't analyzed your market.

Who are your competitors, your prospective suppliers, your potential customers? You may be a flexible, lean start-up, but how can you take advantage of your adaptability if you don't understand the environment you're adapting to? We talked earlier about identifying your customer segments and competitors, but it's time to dig deeper into that analysis and look also at the broader task of analyzing your industry and the macro environment you're operating in.

Understanding the dynamics and the who's who within your market is essential. You need to know who the other companies in your space are, what they're about, who's running them, and their price points. Do you think executives at Coca-Cola don't study Pepsi?

If you're a particularly spunky entrepreneur, perhaps you're thinking, "I'm going to revolutionize my industry, so this analysis is pointless." Let's say you're right. Do you have a view on how your market and industry will look once you burst onto the scene and lay it to waste? If not, then this analysis is still worthwhile. If you're anticipating some dramatic victorious emergence from the chaos in a straight-from-Hollywood fashion, we humbly suggest you reconsider the likelihood of that eventuality.

If you want to build trust with investors, it is important to:

- Have an estimated value of the size of the market for your product/solution, often referred to as the total addressable market, or TAM, and a clear definition of your initial target customer(s) within that market.
- Know all your major competitors, especially how their business model (i.e., how they make money) is like and different from yours.
- Understand the relative strength of the forces beyond your control that are shaping your industry.

Since you don't want to be caught flat-footed, how can you bring your knowledge up to par? Let's take a high-level run through the basics of clarifying your business strategy, identifying the internal points of value in your company, and understanding your external environment. If you want further guidance on the concepts below, we have provided some options in our resource pages at the end of this book.

Universe of Competitors

You'll need to determine your universe of competitors and chart out each one's management team, investors, capital raised, revenues, valuations, acquisitions, product/service offerings, key suppliers, market niche, price band, major customers, and any other useful information you can (legally) acquire.

Any company in your market or offering a substitute should be included in this analysis. You must understand who's doing things like you, their success in raising money and generating revenues, and the pool of early-stage investors that have willingly doled out cash to participants in your industry.

Depending on your industry, you might be able to source a wealth of knowledge from free public sources through standard internet searches. Others might require you to use a paid service such as PitchBook to get specific information. In addition, you must check out your competitors' social media pages (including LinkedIn), and actively monitor their online presence and activity to get a clearer picture of how to differentiate your product or service and brand.

Ideally, you'll put all this competitive research in a single document that your management team can readily reference. You should also have a clear plan for who is responsible for updating this document. The last thing you want is version control issues (which even large companies can struggle with) that may lead you to botch an important fact (e.g., that a competitor is running a promotional sale campaign when in fact that campaign ended eight months ago).

The updating process should be periodic (e.g., quarterly), so that you stay on top of your market's composition. Committing to periodic updates doesn't mean you can't make updates immediately as new information comes in. It just ensures that someone is doing a thorough market scan at least once every review period.

Product-Market Fit

Clear product-market fit emerges when the solution to the problem solved by your product is one your target customers are willing to pay for. People are willing to pay for something when they prefer your company's solution to available alternatives.

Put another way, product-market fit is established when a market of consumers demanding your product is large enough that your company will be able to generate sustained sales at an economically viable level. This means it isn't enough to have built a great piece of technology; people must actually want to buy your product implementing that technology.

Therefore, it is vital to understand how your company creates value, which is difficult to do without understanding the dynamics of your market. All the research and analysis we describe below, focused on understanding your potential customer market, will help you assess the product-market fit potential of your offering.

Analyzing your competitors helps you understand customers' other options, what they are responding to, and what features of your product may or may not be popular. These insights will help you adjust your product's features to attract more customers. (Attracting more customers means you're improving your product-market fit.)

Beyond competitor research you'll need to engage directly with target customers to evaluate demand for your product and their overall satisfaction with the offering. Engaging with customers is key to understanding whether your product's capabilities and features are likely to drive consumer adoption.

It is so important to achieve product-market fit that we recommend working at it until you have evidence that your product provides a solution to the problem that target customers are willing to pay to solve, and that they prefer your company's solution to available alternatives. If you can't articulate what this evidence is, you will struggle to raise money, as investors will find it impossible to chart your growth path to profitability.

Before you move into stage two to prepare for the raise, you must be confident that what you're raising money for is a product sufficiently demanded at an economically viable price point. Put another way, you must be comfortable that your idea can support a commercially viable business given the industry and macro environment it will be operating in.

Looking Inside

Let's take a brief look at some analytical frameworks used to think about businesses and how they fit in their market among competitors.

Business Model

First up, the business model. Regardless of how you make money, your business probably relies on one of two business models: differentiation or cost-leadership. Either you're selling a product with distinct features as compared to your competitors or the market, or you're selling a comparable product or service at a lower price point. That's your starting point. Be clear about which one you're pursuing and hammer it home; it's your basis for establishing a competitive advantage.

Don't get distracted by discussions about business models related to pricing (freemium, bundling, etc.), advertising, or party-to-party descriptions (business-to-business, business-to-consumer, etc.). Each of those models is built on top of the fundamental choice of whether you aim to outcompete on price point or with snazzy differentiation to attract customers. Once you figure that out, you're more equipped to answer specific questions about how you'll make and sell your product, and which customers will pay for it.[4]

Competitive Advantage

A competitive advantage is the use of a company's resources and capabilities to sustainably earn above-average profits in an industry. Resources can include the following:

- Human capital (knowledge and experience, technical talent, etc.)
- Intangibles (personal networks into critical components of the customer segment, etc.)
- Unregistered intellectual property (source code, trade secrets, etc.)
- Registered intellectual property (patents, trademarks, copyrights)

Capabilities are based on tacit knowledge, know-how, or skills. They emerge over time as they are developed. If your company's resources and capabilities are valuable, rare, costly to imitate, and organized in a way that your company can exploit, then they can be a source of competitive advantage. Yes, this is a lot of jargon, but if you think about it, you'll see an organized system for understanding, protecting, and developing your company's most valuable features.

SWOT Analysis

There is a good chance you have already done a SWOT (pronounced "swat") analysis before, perhaps in a high school classroom. If you haven't, the basics behind the analysis are to list out the Strengths, Weaknesses, Opportunities, and Threats relevant to your company when considering a course of action. It's best if you apply this analysis to a specific goal (or milestone) your company is trying to achieve: Do your company's S, W, O, and T make it an advisable milestone to pursue?

STRENGTHS	**WEAKNESSES**
• Strength 1 • Strength 2	• Weakness 1 • Weakness 2
OPPORTUNITIES	**THREATS**
• Opportunity 1 • Opportunity 2	• Threat 1 • Threat 2

Chart out your SWOT box as above, with one rectangle subdivided into four smaller rectangles, one for each category. Then review your entries in each box, write up your conclusions, and use them to inform your strategic decisions and path forward. We've included links to some great templates in our resources section at the end of this book.

Value Chain Analysis

A typical value chain breaks a company down into its core functions to analyze where value is created and destroyed in each business process. Your core functions are those involved in transforming your business's inputs into outputs and collecting payment from customers. In this context, the "value" created along the chain of processes is the customers' willingness to pay for the final product, which, if you like money, must be higher than the input costs (labor, software subscriptions, rent, etc.).

When designing your product, consider dimensions that add value: unique product features, unique product performance, exceptional customer service, reliability and durability, variety within your product offerings, availability/scarcity, customizability, and brand perception (i.e., prestige). Look through some sample value chains for companies in your industry to get a sense of what these should look like. More on this topic is available in our resources section.

The World around You

Part of charting a path for growth is understanding the broader environment in which you and your competitors exist. Porter's Five Forces and PESTLE analyses are two ways to build that understanding. The former, created by Harvard professor Michael Porter, is useful for analyzing the industry environment, and the latter, for the macro environment (i.e., the world around the industry).

Porter's Five Forces

Porter's Five Forces is a classic framework you can use to understand the forces at play in your industry and the possibility for establishing a competitive advantage. If one of the forces is particularly strong, it may be more difficult than you expect to carve out a competitive advantage, earn above-average profits, and ultimately realize a level of growth that warrants venture investors' interest.

Here is a quick run-down of the "five forces" shaping the competitive dynamics of your industry. They are (1) rivalry among competing firms, (2) bargaining power of customers, (3) bargaining power of suppliers, (4) threat of new entrants, and (5) threat of substitutes. If you analyze the restaurant industry using this framework, you'll notice that customers have lots of choices, competition is brutal, and potential customers can always cook at home if nothing satisfies them. Given all that, you can see why it is extremely challenging to build a competitive advantage in that industry. Because the threat of substitutes is high, so is the bargaining power of consumers and the level of industry rivalry.

When analyzing your own industry, you'll want to understand how you can manage these forces to better position yourself for competitive success. There are many articles online that detail how to do this analysis. We've provided links to some of these in our resources section.

PESTLE Analysis

The world outside of your industry affects your business, too. This is the "macro" environment. You can assess how your business is affected by the macro environment through broader lenses using a PESTLE analysis. (The previous version of this acronym, PEST, is now outdated but was more memorable!) Specifically, you analyze the impact of Political, Economic, Social, Technological, Legal/regulatory, and Environmental factors on your business.

Depending on your industry, the different factors' relevancy will vary. Each factor is made up of several subfactors. For example, some economic factors to consider may include national GDP growth rates, exchange rates, interest rates, inflation (or deflation) rates, disposable income, unemployment rates, labor force participation, and so on. Again, there are lots of helpful resources online if you want to undertake a PESTLE analysis, so we've kept this description brief and included some recommended resources at the end of this book.

Rinse and Repeat

Sadly, you're unlikely to get away with doing these analyses once. At least in the future, you'll (hopefully) have more people you can delegate to and you won't be starting from scratch. Reviewing your business model and understanding your value chain, your strengths, weaknesses, opportunities, and threats, as well as the forces defining your industry, is a continuous process. Never stop reflecting on these analyses—and your own frameworks, too—and using them to frame your thinking about ways to improve your business. Never stop comparing yourself to your competitors either, as you need to deliver more value than they do. How can you if you don't understand what they're doing?

Blown Raise Story: Market Sizing

This story is brief, and so was the amount of time investors spent on this entrepreneur's pitch. An entrepreneur created a wellness product targeting patients who were currently taking a specific drug. As the entrepreneur assembled his pitch deck for investors (see chapter 10), he included data on how many people were taking the drug and how much money the company could make if they captured just a small percentage of these individuals. The big problem? He had put in ten times the sales figures, and the error flowed through to all his projections.

The investors knew it was an error. The drug was produced by a large public company that provided granular quarterly disclosures on the drug's sales, so they were able to verify the real number. It turns out the entrepreneur was using a dated figure from an old investor presentation that the pharmaceutical company had put out more than five years ago. Since then, the drug's patent had expired and there were several generic low-cost alternatives available in the market.

When the investors asked the entrepreneur to "clarify" the figure, the entrepreneur doubled down and said the patient figure was correct because he got it from the company that produced the drug. When investors realized that this wasn't a simple typo, and that the entrepreneur genuinely believed the erroneous figure, which was so critical to understanding his market, they quickly passed.

You've finished stage one, the ideation phase, which begins when an entrepreneur commits to advancing an idea as a business. Before you move on to stage two, reflect on how important it is to clearly articulate how your company makes money. Once you can do that, make sure you have the other basics under your belt: know who your competitors are and how you're different, take necessary steps protect your intellectual property, set up your legal structure and understand the legal framework related to your business, and accept that you almost certainly will lose some degree of control over your business. Once you've done all these things and have a clear understanding of your industry environment, you're ready for stage two: preparation for the raise.

STAGE TWO

PREPARATION

A PERSON WITH a good idea who foregoes other opportunities (such as a full-time job) and commits fully to building that idea into a successful business is a diamond in the rough. These rare and daring folks are convinced that the considerable challenges are worth facing, and that their pursuit is where they should focus their time and energy.

Now is when entrepreneurs must prepare themselves for hard questions. It is no small task to translate an idea and passion into a sensible financial story that demonstrates the value of the business and compels investors to write checks. It takes a lot of preparation. You must also accept the limits of your own abilities, determine who else is needed, and learn how to motivate them.

After laying the necessary groundwork in the ideation phase, but before pitching investors, you must consolidate and document your thoughts into a set of organized materials that explain the company and its vision in a compelling and professional manner. To be prepared for questioning and present as a diligent, prudent, and trustworthy steward of funds, you must reflect on several matters before jumping into pitches. You want to show up to your meetings with a balanced, incentivized, and cohesive team (or a plan to build one), a data room, a pitch deck, a financial model, clear understanding of your key performance metrics, and the necessary professional advice.

The last thing you want is to blow the presentation by not understanding the process well enough and, despite all your hard work, being unprepared to clearly present critical information and answer routine questions. Let's review how to ensure you'll show up prepared.

6

Good Friends Aren't Always Good Business Partners

MANY MANAGEMENT teams at new companies first coalesce because the founders happen to be close friends or colleagues. There's nothing wrong with that. When it can be wrong is when no one on your management team works well together or has the skills your company needs to succeed (which often isn't uncovered until after you've started). It's great that your co-founder Jim can do a keg stand, but can he write a marketing plan? Please don't let yourself get caught in the trap of working with only people you already know. If you find yourself in this situation, and it isn't working, you must act quickly to address it.

One of the biggest mistakes a founder can make when seeking capital is to underestimate the importance of the management team to investors and the ultimate success of the business. Effective management teams are a key differentiator between successful companies and dumpster fires. Sophisticated investors know this; it isn't their first rodeo.

After meeting hundreds of management teams, investors develop an eye for identifying gong shows, and if your team gives off the vibe that you are anything but consummate professionals, you're done. After all, investors will consider putting their money at risk only because of their desire to make more.

Without a cohesive management team armed with the necessary skills, experience, and attitude, how can investors possibly believe that the business will ever succeed? We'll save you the guess—they can't. Investors must trust that your team can handle and deploy their money like professionals and grow the business to the degree they expect.

Recognize Who You're Missing and What You Need Them For

When first assembling your team, you may be one of the lucky few able to aggregate a group of exceptional and well-balanced specialists. It's possible one of your co-founders has built three companies, your chief technology officer has twenty-five years of experience, and your head of sales has structured and managed sales departments at a start-up from founding to exit and two blue chip companies, but probably not. Chances are you're missing some type of expertise on your bench. That's okay, that's normal.

Before meeting with investors, be aware of your team's strengths and where you need to shore up the line. It is common for investors to ask who you need to bring in following their investment, and you need a ready response. For example, you may say, "We need a full-time chief technology officer as our patent portfolio continues to scale," or "We have an exceptional founding team for product design, but as we prepare to go to market later this year, we will need people to help us with both marketing and supply chain management." If you believe you have a stacked deck, be ready to justify that belief.

As with every answer to a potential investor, be concise and to the point. Give a supporting rationale phrased in a way that conveys you're confident you know what you need but open to the investor's input on your plan. These signaling efforts will pay off after dozens (potentially hundreds) of pitches to investors by subtly demonstrating you are a decisive but cooperative person open to advice and suggestions, which will help start the trust train rolling.

Be Realistic about Each Team Member's Level of Commitment

Nearly every great human accomplishment involved a team. If a team cannot stick together through tough times (and we mean gut-wrenching times), it probably won't achieve anything amazing. In a start-up, it is as certain as death and taxes that teams will face *really* tough times.

A team must start on the right foot. This means that everyone's expectations of one another should be crystal clear. Each person must commit to meeting the expectations others have of them. If you know people expect more of you than you are willing to give, be a good sport and get off the field. Doing anything else is selfish and will only create problems down the road, perhaps even in the middle of a raise.

If someone on your team values going on an annual fishing trip every May—come hell or high water—you should be aware of that, because you have no idea what could happen next spring. Maybe you can live with it, maybe you can't, but you should have complete clarity. If someone has only worked in a large bureaucratic institution with lots of support staff and held senior roles, but will now be taking on a relatively junior role, or has spent most of their working life at an academic institution or in the public sector, be very clear when it comes to expectations for commitment and responsibility for task completion.

Building a company simply isn't a nine-to-five job, and no one can wait for "someone else" to handle something. The pace is fast, the burden is heavy, and the clock doesn't stop for leaders. We've seen companies stall out because people from the aforementioned backgrounds were not clear-eyed about what was going to be required of them in a start-up context.

Clearly Delineate Roles and Responsibilities and Properly Delegate Authority at the Executive Level

Investors want to know who is in charge. They don't want cute answers such as "We make all decisions together." That may have worked for you so far, but investors don't like unnecessary risks. As your company scales, unless there is a compelling reason for co-CEOs (there likely isn't), investors will probably pour cold water on shared final decision-making authority. To most investors, that approach falls nicely in the category of unnecessary risk.

Instead, investors prefer a governance structure that clearly allocates ultimate decision-making powers to avoid deadlocks. This doesn't mean you can't take an extreme anti-hierarchy approach among the ranks, but at the very least, responsibilities and authority should be clearly delineated among executives.

Building a company is a daily adventure. You can never foresee the decisions you'll have to make—it's like parenting with (multiple) platonic partners. If your venture suddenly grinds to a halt because there is disagreement among the proverbial co-CEOs, the consequence is this: your company shifts focus to internal politics instead of developing its products and services and focusing on its growth plan. Meanwhile, your competitors keep moving ahead. Put another way: your competitive position is exposed, you fall behind, and investors' trust in you is eroded because indecision has affected their potential returns. Because the indecision stemmed from strife among management, investors will assign a higher likelihood to this happening again (which could sabotage your next round of fundraising).

Part of avoiding clashes of authority is having clearly defined roles and responsibilities among management. You want to know who is doing what and why. There are many views on organizational design (e.g., hierarchical versus flat structures), but you need to decide what works for you and work diligently to implement it. Knowing who is doing what and why is just the start.

You need to track and assess people's competence and development. This is somewhat obvious, but people will struggle to clearly assign roles on their own, especially when companies grow quickly. To minimize the potential for conflict, it is important to give folks clarity and communicate openly and consistently with your management team about roles and responsibilities. People need to know who they report to and who is responsible for assigning them tasks.

Keep Your Head Out of the Sand

For a myriad of reasons, the last decade or so has seen the rise of an acute and vocal focus (including by investors) on the human elements of companies. The adage that corporations exist only to drive shareholder profits is now largely passé in most circles (even under some laws). It would be irresponsible not to mention one component of this transition that will likely arise during your raise: diversity and inclusion. We won't tread far into waters we're unequipped for, but the evolving perspective on businesses' role in society has a lot to say about designing workforces and related policies.

While most major metropolitan areas in the United States and Canada are exceptionally racially and ethnically diverse, it's not guaranteed that a board, management team, or employee base will organically realize a diverse composition. Companies with no women or members of minority groups will not play well in some investor circles (and may not reap the practical benefits that have been shown to flow from assembling a diverse team). At some point a non-diverse company will likely be asked why it is lacking in diversity, and some investors, on this basis alone, will refuse to give that company funding.

Don't get tripped up because of your blind spot, and don't be upset that you have one—we all do. When we first made our list of "testers" to review our draft chapters of this book (to make sure they made sense and were readable), we didn't even think about diversity because our social and professional networks run the gamut of race and ethnicity.

However, we stepped back and realized that we had inadvertently selected 90 percent men and just 10 percent women to read our work. We felt a little sheepish and focused on balancing out the list before adding more dudes.

The point is, we knew enough to check for and correct bias. You shouldn't be afraid to check whether any unconscious biases have bled into your team's composition. Aside from the benefits that have been shown to flow from diverse teams, as a practical matter, some sources of funding are available only if your company satisfies necessary diversity and inclusion criterion. You're only human and we all have biases. The question is whether we're secure enough to recognize and adjust for them.

The rising focus on the conscience of companies also brings in considerations beyond diversity and inclusion. Depending on your business, socially conscious behavior may tie into brand management that is integral to your corporate strategy. It is worth remembering that your company is a social participant with its own identity, and the perception of that identity can have a significant effect on your bottom line and ability to raise money.

We want you to put a lot of thought into composing your management team, because the membership will be the limiting factor in that team's success. You want skilled people who have a history of cooperating with others and identifying and fixing problems.

7

Organizations Need Organization

THIS IS a bit of a common-sense chapter, but it needs to be said: without taking organization seriously, a company will not be an organization. It will be merely a collection of thoughts and initiatives in disarray, for which raising money may become a pipe dream.

To start your own business, you need to collect, record, and organize an inordinate amount of information. Details of competitors, customer contracts, supplier contracts, advisor contracts and materials, product design plans, patent filings—the list can go on and on. This information will be sourced from a breadth of different parties and publications, many of which may even come to different conclusions about various matters. If there are major differences, you will want an organized means to recognize and resolve those differences.

You will be assigning innumerable tasks. Some will be done by individual team members, while others require a collaborative effort. Collaboration involves coordinating schedules, setting deadlines, formalizing agendas and action lists, and defining ultimate deliverables. You will need a system to organize which tasks have been completed, which are mission critical, and which can be deferred. The last thing you want is to book an investor meeting for Monday, only to afterwards realize a key deliverable wanted for that meeting won't be ready on time, or that the CEO has been double-booked with another investor.

In fast-moving industries, new information is being produced constantly, and it can sometimes dramatically affect your business model or financial potential. If a new regulation or law is introduced in your industry (very common with rapidly evolving industries), you must be aware of it and incorporate that information into your materials and business plan. It will hurt your odds if you aren't up to speed about a key development your prospective investors want to know about or you don't refresh your materials, and let them go "stale."

Some Basics of Organization

Here are some fundamental things you can do to immediately improve your organization and productivity:

- Keep a clean and dedicated workspace.
- Break goals and milestones into discrete tasks.
- Track your progress in writing on particular action items.
- Use a calendar to allocate your time to task areas.
- Turn off your phone when you need to focus.
- Keep your emails organized in appropriate folders.

Software programs, such as monday.com, can also be implemented to help you manage enterprise activities. Make use of project management aids like Gantt charts.

Organize to Impress

Executive teams that win over investors always demonstrate organization. They have an absolute command of information relevant to their business. Such teams speak intelligently about their industry, their competitors, and what makes their company stand out. While some people are gifted with photographic memories, they'll still need to be organized to present that known information to others. Most of us mere mortals need to carefully catalog the information we gather and study it to present it confidently, so spend time doing so.

If you went into an investor pitch and stated your industry has grown at 120 percent per year for the last three years, your investor will likely ask about that number. If you can't recall where you read it or who wrote it, and instead say simply that you found the number over the course of "your research," you may rock their confidence. For all the investor knows, you got that number from a source with zero credibility, or even worse, you just made it up. We don't want this to happen to you, so be organized and know your sources.

Raising Money Is Stressful Enough, Don't Let Disorganization Make It Worse

The list of things you should not do if you want to be and appear organized is endless, but for the sake of brevity, here are a few pitfalls to avoid:

- Scattering documents across different cloud providers or data centers without clear labeling and a centralized indexing system.
- Showing up to meetings or working discussions unprepared.
- Rejecting the use of a calendar and instead having faith in yourself to remember your schedule.

Building a company is emotionally taxing and can be so stressful it affects your physical and mental well-being—and capital raises are particularly stressful. Organizational skills can reduce stress, so bring an organizationally tinted lens to everything you do. Whether it is managing your personal life, a product development timeline, or a meeting, applying principles and methods of organization can bring down the stress level. You need this, and your loved ones will thank you, too.

Though people organize things in their own ways, some people's systems are better than others. There are big differences between people's ability to organize themselves (e.g., a hoarder vs. a librarian), and there are nuanced differences between people on par with one another, too (e.g., successful lawyer A vs. successful lawyer B). In the latter case, each lawyer has equal opportunity to become more organized by observing the habits of the other lawyer and, where it is helpful and compatible with their own habits, layering in the other's methods.

If you are working with excellent managers, learn from them. Talk to them about how they organize themselves for work. Yes, it is a silly conversation topic to have at such a general level—something like "what categories do you create in Outlook" isn't exactly fun office chat—but real efficiency benefits can accrue if managers and employees foster a culture that values efforts to be more organized whether by employee practices or implementation of technology solutions.

Make More Money per Unit of Effort

Being organized is all about making it easier to do value-add tasks when you need to and ensuring you spend as little time as possible on the logistics of starting, switching between, or gathering the necessary materials for tasks. By minimizing wasted time, you're freeing up more opportunities for value-add activities. In the context of a capital raise, being organized can make the difference between a reasonably intense experience and a nightmare. Organization will help your capital raise specifically, but the benefits are essentially endless for your broader business operation, too.

The HEXACO Personality Inventory dimension of conscientiousness (the category most closely associated with business success) is most positively associated with perfectionism, prudence, diligence, and organization. Clearly, organization is not without importance. Without organization being applied as a guiding principle across your company, success may be compromised. The finances could end up a mess, and you may end up overpaying or underpaying taxes, which in either case affects cash flow planning.

Alternatively, you could find yourself in disputes with vendors where there is no binding agreement in place. You could inadvertently drive customers nuts by failing to respond in a timely fashion to their complaints. Imagine that a customer who is disappointed in a malfunctioning product calls for a replacement, and ends up waiting for weeks or months (or the replacement never comes). Now imagine they couldn't even get a customer service agent on the phone! They will be doubly angry. These problems stem from poorly planned and unorganized product exchange processes. Sadly, you will lose that customer, and you may inadvertently create an adverse brand ambassador who is very vocal on social media. Being organized hits the bottom line, so always learn from others and ask yourself how you can be more organized in every facet of your business.

8

Get Professional Legal and Financial Advice

IN A company's earliest stages, entrepreneurs can tend to view lawyers, accountants, and intellectual property professionals (also usually lawyers) as opportunists out to bleed them dry, siphon value, and take advantage of their innovative genius. Four hundred dollars or more for just *one* hour of their time? Ridiculous!

If this is how you feel, take a step back. A lot of time and attention goes into starting, raising money for, and running a company properly, and the potential liability associated with doing so improperly drives a premium on the value of high-quality services. If you race off without the right advice, you may find yourself in an inordinate amount of trouble, and the worst part is, you probably won't realize how much trouble you're in until you're neck deep in it.

It can be easy to run afoul of securities laws (the ones that cover raising money, among other things), tax authorities, and any other law, person, or agency you don't realize exists or you have crossed if you don't get the right advice. (For an idea of what documents in a start-up's life cycle are involved, see the Path to Closing diagram at the end of chapter 29.)

Professionals can be very useful when you are raising money, and competent ones can lower your stress level significantly. They can clearly explain options, what is required of you for best practices, and where you may find efficiencies that you were previously unaware of. Even if you don't realize it at the time, their value can be tremendous, and it's better to make your peace with this. After all, they wouldn't charge those rates if people were unwilling to pay them.

Engage legal and financial professionals early, communicate with them regularly, and preview your plans with them to head off issues. It is *always* cheaper to do something right the first time than to call an audible halfway down the field, mid-play. We understand it can seem like a daunting task to hire professionals. It's true they are relatively expensive for a company just getting started, and honestly, they do all look the same from the outside looking in. Still, when you hire professionals:

- **Don't delay.** The best professionals do not always have the bandwidth to take on new clients at the drop of a hat. Engage professionals before you race off to meet with investors. Tell them your plans so those professionals can evaluate whether they can take you on as a client and, if so, plan to accommodate you when you need them. Keeping them up to date will help you achieve your desired timeline in a raise.
- **Don't hire someone just because you know them, especially if you haven't worked with them before.** While it is important to like people you work with, a person's work-self can deviate wildly from what they describe or what you expect, so be wary of hiring people just because you know

and like them. Realistically, it is unlikely the person you happen to know is the professional best suited to handle your specific needs. Your friend may be a perfectly competent lawyer or accountant, but lawyers and accountants who specialize in your needs and your industry could be superior. The point is, don't hire someone just because it's easy. Do a little research, and don't be shy about asking for references. Real professionals will happily offer them up; questionable folks will be offended, grumble, and try to steamroll you into ponying up a retainer or signing an engagement letter.

- **Don't assume bigger is always better or smaller is always cheaper.** There are many highly qualified professionals working in small firms who are just as incentivized to deliver exceptional client services as their counterparts at larger firms. At the same time, although big firms have higher hourly rates, they also tend to see more transaction volume, which often translates into greater efficiency. In other words, a higher hourly rate multiplied by fewer hours may equal a lower total bill than that from a smaller firm. The key element in either case is experience—don't hire a firm that doesn't regularly work with start-ups and doesn't have the scope of specializations (corporate, intellectual property, employment, securities, etc.) that start-ups need. If you don't go to one firm that can do all these things, then you will need to engage multiple firms, and you will be responsible for ensuring they are all equally informed of your business's goings on. All of this will add to your workload.
- **Be sure to negotiate price and method of payment.** Almost everything is negotiable. Tell the professional your circumstances and see what they are open to in terms of

compensation. Some may be willing to accept equity in lieu of cash, and some will adjust their rates or even defer payments until you close your round. Others won't. Keep in mind that some firms are keen to accommodate entrepreneurs where they can, because they recognize that if you are successful in raising capital and building your business, you will require more services they can also provide. Also, don't assume you have to pay the billable hour—ask for flat fees and you may get them in certain circumstances. Make sure to ask the timing increment the lawyer bills in, too. Is it six-minute increments, fifteen-minute increments, or something else? The difference adds up.

You want a lawyer you can work with and who communicates well. In the legal world, "communicates well" means they help you figure out how to do what you want rather than throw cold water on your ideas. If you're lucky, they'll educate you along the way, too. You may also want them to have an office nearby, if you're the type who prefers to meet in person. Side note: meeting with your lawyer regularly can help you save money. Legal issues become expensive when they're neglected. You'll address them sooner the more regularly you speak with your lawyer, which is likely to save you money in the long run.

As a final consideration, it is worth assessing whether they may be able to introduce you to a broader network of folks who could be valuable resources, such as other investors, service providers, or potential hires. This intangible element is likely to come packaged with firms that regularly work on the start-up scene and make it a focus of their business model.

Know When You Need Advice and Listen to It

Remember, you need advice well before you start talking to investors. Professionals handle capital raise processes for a living, so they can ensure you're packaging everything (pitch decks, business plans, legal documents, etc.) to build investor confidence and establish trust that your management team will handle investors' money with the care it deserves. Such professionals will also ensure you don't violate securities laws or commit some other faux pas.

There is no point in paying for advice if you aren't going to listen to and consider it. You don't have to follow every piece of advice, but if you're not actually weighing the merits or taking the advice a reasonable portion of the time, then you are wasting your money.

Unless you're a former capital markets guru, there should be no doubt in your mind that experienced professionals know more about raising money than you do. That's okay, they're supposed to! Your job is to know your company and communicate your objectives to your professionals so they can help you present the best version of your company to investors and manage the risks related to the financing.

It is less than ideal when an attorney suggests something you ignore and, as a result, you end up facing a needless liability or lost opportunity. Take what your advisors say seriously. If you're going to disregard their advice, have a good reason for doing so and explain it to them. When you do, you may find they can highlight other points of consideration you were previously unaware of that could affect your final decision.

Know When to Fire a Professional

Whether you find it easy or difficult to hire a professional, knowing when to fire them is another matter. Some general indications that the relationship isn't working and that a frank conversation is required are: (1) you frequently need them to clarify what they are saying (they aren't speaking to you in a way you understand); (2) they are consistently missing deadlines, avoiding calls, or failing to respond to emails; and (3) they are unorganized, waste your time on calls, and send bills that include time spent on tasks that seem grossly out of sync with the amount of time the task should have taken (though people do often underestimate how long tasks take to do properly).

The best way to avoid these issues is to ask for references before engaging a professional. Discuss your expectations with them and record that conversation in an email separate from the engagement letter. Even if you make all these efforts, the professional you choose could still be much better or worse than you expected. Until you work with someone, you never really know what you are going to get, so you must remain ready to fire them if needed.

9

Ready a Data Room

IF AN investor is compelled by your pitch and wants to dig deeper, a common follow-up request is, "Can I get access to your data room?" If your response is anything other than a clear yes (subject to them signing a non-disclosure agreement), then you've already made a serious error, which we want to help you avoid. And please, don't respond with, "What is a data room?" You'll only be making things worse.

When you pitch an investor, you will inevitably make several claims about your company, your team, and what you plan on doing. Most investors who hear your pitch will take a "trust but verify" approach when listening. This means they will assume what you claim in your pitch is true, but will want to confirm that the information you have presented is genuine. This is where the data room comes in.

A data room is essentially a big folder containing various subfolders organized in a coherent manner, which contains all the documents and other information relevant to your business. It should include all the information an investor may want to review to confirm that your business is real and that the claims you made in your mesmerizing pitch are genuine. We use the term "data room" because in the pre-internet and pre-digital era, these folders were housed in a physical room, where folks gathered to enjoy quiet moments of review.

These days, almost all data rooms exist entirely online, and many emerging companies upload and store their key documents on something as accessible as Google Drive or Dropbox. More mature companies tend to use professional data room services, such as Datasite, iDeals, Firmex, or Intralinks, which create indexes of contents, track user access, identify which documents have been opened and by whom, and stamp digital watermarks on documents downloaded from the data room. These are safeguards to stop people from doing shady things when given access to confidential information.

Regardless of which service is used, any entrepreneur who wants to raise money must provide a way for investors to expeditiously verify their claims by reviewing the company's documents, so you must set up a data room.

What to Put in Your Data Room

Knowing you need a data room isn't helpful if you don't know what to put in it. If you did an internet search for "what should I put in my data room," you were probably aghast at how many documents you "should" assemble. Some lists recommend uploading several hundred documents, including detailed financial results from the past several years. You would be right to scratch your head and wonder how anyone expects you to upload several years of financial results if your company has existed for less than a year. The answer is: they don't. Whatever list you stumbled upon was probably not prepared for someone in your circumstances.

Data rooms are not unique to early-stage companies raising their first few rounds of capital. They are also assembled by the world's largest companies when going through capital raises, mergers and acquisitions, and other special situations. The number of documents and the level of detail you need to provide in your data room hinges on the nature of the contemplated transaction and your business's stage in its life cycle.

With that in mind, regardless of the size of your company or the amount of money being sought, there are certain documents that even the newest companies should include:

- **Corporate records.** Investors (specifically, their lawyers) need to verify that your company has a legal existence. The documents proving this will vary depending on the legal structure you have selected for your business and its jurisdiction of formation. For example, if your business is a corporation, the lawyers will want to see the articles of incorporation, bylaws, any (unanimous) shareholders agreement, details of previous share transfers, the share register, and copies of all directors' and shareholders' written resolutions and meeting minutes.
- **Employment agreements and personnel details.** Investors are really betting on people in a start-up, so they want to know more about the people they are entrusting to steward their capital and those people's arrangements with the company. While the description you gave in your pitch deck for your chief marketing officer as an "SEO Ninja" was captivating, you must flesh that out for investors and clarify how your team is incentivized to see the company succeed. It is a must to upload biographies and signed employment agreements for key personnel.
- **Business plan.** Undoubtedly your sleek and sexy pitch deck has fantastically explained how you will provide a great product or service and make everyone involved rich

along the way, but most investors want a bit more meat on the bone. This document should clearly lay out your substantive and specific plan and timeline for the business's growth and path to profitability.

As your business charts its path toward maturity and you raise ever more capital for world domination, you will receive more robust requests for documentation in your data room. To start, investors will want details of your financial performance, copies of material contracts, proof that you own the substantive assets (tangible and intangible) you claim ownership of, and details around any litigation your company is embroiled in. Of course, this isn't an exhaustive set list. They'll ask for whatever they need to trust you have an acceptable chance of making them money.

A simple rule to determine what you need to upload is to ask yourself whether providing a specific document will help verify information important to making an investment decision. If you said you executed a lucrative contract with a major customer, investors will want to review the signed contract to understand its terms. If you claim to have poached a top-notch VP from one of your competitors to run your marketing strategy, investors will want to review that person's employment agreement.

If you are ever uploading information about your company's intellectual property to your data room (patent filings, research-in-progress, design drawings, etc.) ALWAYS consult with your intellectual property lawyer (and if you don't have one, get one) about proper disclosure and best practices for access BEFORE uploading anything. You can tell that this is a serious matter because this is the only bolded section in the book.

Organization Is Key

Mislabeled documents, illogically titled and unorganized subfolders, outdated financials, draft and undated versions of contracts that were never executed, and missing items will all affect your credibility during a capital raise. It is hardly a stretch to imagine that an investor may doubt an entrepreneur's ability to build a business empire if they cannot even organize a series of folders and their contents with weeks, if not months, to prepare.

If you have never assembled a data room, there are simple procedures you can follow to make sure yours appears professional and polished:

1. **Identify and name.** First, identify what documents you need to collect. We have provided links to useful lists of items to upload in our resources section, but as mentioned, always consider your own unique situation. When in doubt, seek advice and get a disclosure list from your lawyer. Also, choose a naming convention and stick with that convention when you name all documents (e.g., "[Document Title] - [Date of Execution]"). "00237ZR.pdf" isn't very helpful to reviewers.

2. **Allocate responsibility.** If you are a one-person operation, you can skip this step, as everything is going to fall on you. If you have a team, you will want to clarify which documents each person is responsible for gathering, naming, and uploading, and who is responsible for the final quality control check before anyone is granted access.

3. **Organize the docs.** Once your documents are identified and gathered, you need to organize them in your folders in a manner that makes it easy for investors to find what they are looking for. This is hardly rocket science, but it

is important to group documents into logically organized and appropriately named folders, which requires time and focus. Even some data rooms prepared by professionals are a disaster. When you encounter thoughtful ones, they stand out—the effort shines through.

4. **Review and update.** Given how quickly your business may evolve, there is a real possibility some of the documents you upload may not jibe with one another. For example, the budget you put into your pitch deck may not match the budget you laid out in the business plan you wrote a few months ago but haven't updated. Always make sure someone reviews all uploaded documents to avoid inconsistencies, duplications, missing items, and other self-inflicted wounds that undermine your credibility. Remember, one of the pillars of conscientiousness, which is so critical to business success, is perfectionism (that means you review your work).

Data Rooms Are Living Places

Fundraising can take a lot of time, during which your business may evolve considerably. Perhaps you land a major customer, one of your patent applications is approved, or one of your colleagues absconds to the mountains to find themselves. It happens.

These changes will make your data room "stale," meaning it no longer reflects the reality of the company you're asking investors to fund. To avoid this potential awkwardness, think of data rooms as living places requiring routine maintenance and attention to stay current with the latest company developments and related documentation. Put another way, you should review and update your data room as events transpire at your company.

Every Investor Focuses on Slightly Different Things

No two investors are the same. You may encounter investors on one end of the spectrum who scrutinize every single document, while others (far less common) are willing to wire you funds after a quick review. You may hear stories from other entrepreneurs who say they didn't bother putting together a data room and had no problem getting money. Ignore these people.

Investors who like your pitch and are hot to invest don't want to request data room access only to hear you haven't prepared one or don't know what they're talking about. They will not be pleased if you ask them to wait a few weeks for it to come together. They'll have moved on by then. Please don't let a lack of preparation signal to investors that you aren't serious about raising money; otherwise, they probably won't trust you with theirs.

Venture Co. Data Room

🗁 Employment Agreements

- ☐ CEO Founder Employment Agreement – Executed – 2023-06-06
- ☐ CTO Founder Employment Agreement – Executed – 2023-06-06
- ☐ Head of Product Employment Agreement – Executed – 2023-06-13

🗁 Organizational Documents

- ☐ Venture Co. – Articles of Incorporation
- ☐ Venture Co. – Share Register

🗁 Business Plan

- ☐ Business Plan – Long Form
- ☐ Business Plan – Executive Summary

10

Prepare a Pitch Deck

ALONG YOUR entrepreneurial journey, you will likely hear well-traveled anecdotes of founders who coaxed an investor to hand over several million dollars after scribbling their business idea on the back of a cocktail napkin. The idea was too compelling to resist! If you believe you can replicate this scenario, you're better advised to pick up some lottery tickets to satisfy your thirst for long shots. Since we want you to succeed, we'd prefer you pass on the cocktail napkin approach and assemble a proper investor presentation instead.

There are a few labels for investor presentations: your "pitch book," "pitch deck," or just "deck." These decks are typically made using presentation software like PowerPoint, Keynote, or Canva, so the builder can include various text and graphical components to tell their company's story. This isn't a white paper, it's more fun! Regardless of what term or software you use, the pitch deck's purpose is to succinctly explain the investment opportunity in a clear way that excites a prospective investor.

Professional investors, who write some of the largest checks, see hundreds of pitches every year. They do not dwell on details until they are sold on the vision and the team. If an investor must scroll through fifteen slides filled with inspirational quotes from Warren Buffett before learning what product or service a company provides, they will probably pass. Longer is not better, especially if what the reader cares about is not on the first slide or two.

What do investors need to see in your deck?

Tell a Story

At its core, an investor presentation is a story.

Great pitch decks take the reader on a journey. They are easy to follow and each page flows logically to the next. You're trying to design the lazy river of reading. Any investor who reads your presentation should clearly understand how your company creates, captures, and delivers value, and feel that betting on your company could make them lots of money. Your goal is to convince them they must hear more from you.

One of the biggest mistakes entrepreneurs make when crafting their presentation is losing perspective of how important it is to paint the big picture for investors. Too often entrepreneurs delve into the nitty-gritty details of their product or service. Entrepreneurs who do this often assume the investor is an expert in the industry, so the business case needs no explanation. They think the investor just needs to see the product or service and they'll understand the big picture!

The problem with this approach is that, even if an investor claims they are an industry expert, it does not mean they will fully understand the economic potential of your specific solution. Just because an investor is an expert in artificial intelligence does not mean they are an expert in the way you are applying it to a specific industry (especially since it's presumably a novel solution). Don't assume what an investor may know. Keep your deck accessible, but be ready to offer more in-depth detail if asked.

Another major problem with failing to focus on the big picture and getting lost in the details is that you will turn off investors who are not experts and can't understand your value proposition. Many angels have made their own money from an unrelated industry (or inherited it), and if you don't make it easy for them, you are only making it harder on yourself.

Create Good Content

Your deck's contents will vary depending on your company's industry, offering, and funding stage. Investors can't exactly expect you to include historical financial results if you are a brand-new enterprise. Nor should they expect to see your company's patent portfolio if the primary reason you're raising funds is to develop patentable technology and commercialize it. That said, investors have common questions they need answered to see your company's potential.

Every deck must articulate what problem you are addressing, how the current solutions to that problem fall short, how your solution better addresses the problem, why funding your solution could earn the investor a great return, and why you're the team to take your solution to market. If any of this sounds familiar, it is because it's the first thing we talked about in chapter one. In essence, you need to remind yourself what motivated you to undertake this venture in the first place and spell it out for investors.

Details on the leadership team who will ultimately manage the investment are essential. The composition and aptitude of your team is a major focus for investors. They know leadership changes over time. Your company will bring in new talent as it matures, but investors need to know the existing team can lead the company through the stage of its life cycle they're being asked to fund.

You also need to state for the reader how much money you want and what you plan to do with it. By no means do you need to provide a line-by-line breakdown (like the $25 a month you are going to spend on a specific software subscription), but you should provide reasonable detail broken down into big buckets conveying how you will allocate their money. For example, you might plan on spending 5 percent of their investment on "digital marketing" over the next twelve months.

In the spirit of making things easy for readers, include contact information. Tell them how to reach you! You don't want an interested party to email the wrong person at your organization or be left trying to connect with you on LinkedIn to book a follow-up meeting. Tell them exactly who they should reach out to at your company and how. If you want to present as a real pro, include a link to your calendar so they can schedule a meeting.

Aesthetics Matter

Books are judged by their covers, and your pitch deck will be scrutinized on its professionalism and aesthetic quality—full stop. You may be in the process of developing a revolutionary product that could make billions, but if your presentation is a hot mess, you will have a harder time raising cash than if you present something polished.

Your pitch deck makes your company's first impression on investors. If a deck is poorly formatted, riddled with typos, contains squished graphics, and is difficult to follow, practically no one will want to invest. Understand, this is not a matter of investors being snobby. Investors will reasonably be concerned if an entrepreneur put so little effort into something as critical to raising money and achieving their dreams as the pitch deck; perhaps that person will apply similar imprudence to running their business.

You do not want to fall into the trap of thinking that, because you are just "starting out" or "in the early stages," you need not pay attention to detail or spend time making your deck look and feel professional. Building your investor presentation is like dressing up for a job interview: you are trying to put your best foot forward. If you are struggling to get started, know that there are a wealth of publicly accessible corporate presentations and pitch decks from companies that successfully raised capital, which you can look to for inspiration and aesthetic guidance. See our resource pages for examples.

Housekeeping Matters

Before you throw down this book, bang out your deck, and fire it out to prospective investors, we have to offer a few warnings.

First, your deck will likely contain projections about the future, such as what you and your team hope to achieve with the money raised. There are certain legal disclaimers you'll want to include. Your deck should include a standalone disclaimer page, ideally placed right after your cover page, warning the reader your presentation contains forward-looking estimates, but that neither you nor your management team are guaranteeing anything. You may feel this is unnecessary because no reasonable investor would assume you can see into the future, but it is necessary.

Another thing to keep in mind as you start distributing your deck is that a fair chunk of the people you send it to are going to share it with other people. It does not matter if you write "Confidential" and "Do not circulate" on every single page—investors have a penchant for sharing decks they receive. Most of these distributions are not intentionally malicious. For example, an investor might want to share your deck with other close investors or a subject-matter expert they trust to gauge whether you are on to something and whether a follow-up meeting with you is worthwhile. Unfortunately, some sharing is intentionally malicious, so try to avoid your deck being the subject of such actions by following the guidance in this chapter.

For this reason, if your company has developed new technologies, patentable inventions, trade secrets, proprietary know-how, or any other form of intellectual property, consult with an intellectual property professional about the level of disclosure appropriate for your deck. The last thing you want is for your company's secret sauce to find its way into the hands of your competitors (or potential competitors) without legal protection.

Must-Have Slides

Regardless of what your company does, how old it is, or what you hope to achieve, we recommend you have slides in your deck that address the following:

- **Value proposition and mission.** What do you want to be and how will you become that?
- **Market opportunity and problem.** What market is your focus and what problem is it facing?
- **Solution.** How are you solving the problem and taking advantage of the opportunity?

- **Product.** What is it and what are its key features?
- **Competitors.** Who are they and how are their products or services different from yours?
- **Unit economics and business model.** How do you (or will you) make money?
- **Market fit and traction with customers.** Who is your customer base and how is it growing?
- **Growth strategy.** What is your road map for growth?
- **Financial ask and use of proceeds.** How much money do you need and what will it be used for?
- **Financial projections.** High-level expectations of sales, expenses, and profits (if any) for three years.
- **Team and advisors.** Who is working with you?
- **Contact information.** How do investors get in touch with you?

11

Build a Financial Model

ANY ENTREPRENEUR serious about raising capital must answer a few threshold questions about the financial specifics of the planned raise before meeting with prospective investors. These include:

- How much money is needed?
- What will that money be spent on? (Commonly referred to as the "use of proceeds.")
- How long until more money is needed?

Having ready answers to these questions is an excellent starting point to boost credibility. We don't want you to be shown the door, so we're telling you this to ensure you won't have to dodge their questions and suggest they focus on the "big picture."

As we discussed, a key component of any funding pitch is a compelling story articulating how your investor can make a great return by investing in your business. You can imagine how difficult it is to estimate an investor's returns if you have not established how much money you need or how you plan to spend it.

To answer these basic questions, you need to document your thoughts on the financial resources necessary, and what they'll be used for, to build your business in the next stage of your vision. Meaning, whether you build it or buy it, you need a financial model.

The Value of Financial Modeling

Sometimes entrepreneurs can be quite cynical about building a financial model for an early-stage round. When you have no revenues, no sales leads, and potentially no working product, building projections for your business several years into the future can justifiably feel like a waste of time.

Investors know you do not have a crystal ball—neither do they. They understand your model will be riddled with assumptions about the future, some of which will be more credible than others. They'll focus on the near-term, predictable elements of your model, rather than long-term projections. For example, your use of proceeds over the next year will receive more scrutiny than your year three revenue projection.

Investors want to see if you have made reasonable assumptions. If you believe you can price your new product at $100, and your competitors price a similar product at $20, your prospective investors will need to hear a strong argument justifying your proposed price. If you think you can reach $500,000 in sales in your first year, investors will want to understand how you plan to hit that number.

If you're unable to spell out these assumptions, you will not help anyone understand the business case and will find yourself further from successful funding. Going through the exercise of building a financial model is tremendously informative. Doing so will help you better understand your business and its potential financial outcomes. It will force you to ask important questions and crystallize your thinking about your business's financial profile.

If you are already asking these questions and collecting assumptions, then you have started on the path to building a financial model. Well done. You're doing yourself a tremendous favor.

Building a Model

For entrepreneurs who have never built a financial model, the prospect of building and presenting one to a professional investor can feel overwhelming. Do not be intimidated! Making a financial model, like any other task, is far easier when you break it down into distinct, actionable steps.

1. Collect assumptions

The first step to building any financial model is identifying the assumptions you'll need to make, collecting supporting data, and establishing supporting rationales. The assumptions you need to make depend on the nature of your business, your industry, and your aspirations for the future, but are related to your unit sales, pricing, variable operating costs, fixed operating costs, and so on. These assumptions can be informed by a variety of sources, including industry reports, news articles, competitors' press releases, professionals (such as lawyers, financial advisors, and accountants), other entrepreneurs, and, most importantly, your own team. These assumptions help inform initial answers to key questions such as salary amounts, office space requirements, product or service launch dates, and marketing costs.

Thinking through the assumptions helps define the details of all the things that must happen for your company to generate revenue, and all the costs to be incurred along the way. This process can be extremely revealing. You might identify additional costs you had not factored into your initial pricing analysis. For example, if you were planning on developing an app to be distributed through the Apple Store, your cost analysis would hopefully include a line item for the 15 to 30 percent cut of sales you pay Apple off the top.

2. Model construction

The next step is constructing the model. If no one on your team has ever built a financial model, the best starting point is to look at other financial models online. Many incubators and accelerators offer up free model templates for entrepreneurs. You can also access templates through services like SlideBean (see also our resource pages for links to a selection of models). Once you sift through a few models, you will notice common themes in organization and mechanics.

For example, many financial models will use different text colors to indicate which numbers are hardcoded and which are calculated from other cells. The use of different colors allows users to know which key assumptions are driving the model and which ones they can change to test different scenarios without breaking the model's logic. In practice, your model might calculate your company's revenue in a period by multiplying your product price by the number of products you believe you can sell in that period. In that case, your product price and number of products sold would be in one color (probably blue), while your revenue figure would be in another color (probably black) representing formula outputs. If you wanted to see the impact of a price change or a swing in sales volume, you would just change the hardcoded numbers in blue or use an appropriate tool to run a scenario analysis.

If you plan to use one of these entrepreneur-friendly prefabricated financial model templates instead of building your own, be wary. By necessity, these models often take a one-size-fits-all approach. That's not a bad thing per se, but it may not be appropriate or optimized for your specific business. Even if the model claims it was designed for a company just like yours, it may be missing some key mechanics that do not capture your company's unique financial profile. These models can be a wonderful starting point, but like anything else, don't unquestionably accept them at face value without considering your proprietary circumstances.

Some entrepreneurs erroneously believe replicating the most complex model they can find online establishes credibility with an investor. However, the best financial model for a pitch is one you understand and can confidently explain. You may be teeing yourself up for embarrassment if you pick an extremely detailed model containing sections you cannot explain. There is also the possibility that, if you present an extremely complex financial model, the investor will not understand it either, which is unlikely to foster an inclination to invest.

3. Review and refine

Once you have a draft financial model, sit down with your team and discuss whether it all makes sense. It is amazing how much your perception of your business can change once you see everything modeled out. Your plans to launch new products might be accelerated, your capital needs might be far less than anticipated, or your product price points may need considerable adjustment to account for your overhead and transaction costs. As you play around with your assumptions, you will start to get a sharper picture of how much money you need, what you will spend it on, and how long it will last, all of which an investor wants to understand.

A Worthy Exercise

As we have belabored, building a financial model, regardless of whether the end product is crude or polished, will be wonderfully informative for an entrepreneur. It forces you to read up on your competitors and your industry, increases your degree of financial fluency, and reveals new considerations. All this learning will increase your confidence and ability to respond to investors' queries, which increases your chances of getting funding.

Blown Raise Story: Merchant Account Madness

An entrepreneur wanted to launch a new events business to host annual expos for fans of the rapidly growing eSports industry. Every event would include celebrity guests, gaming tournaments, and trade booths where companies would be invited to set up and sell products.

He modeled out his forecasted revenues and expenses, calculating that if he sold all the event tickets, he could generate $900,000 in revenue compared to an all-in cost of $400,000 to host the expo. Knowing the idea was risky, the entrepreneur realized that by pre-selling tickets to the event he could reduce the amount of money he would need to raise. If he pre-sold just one-third of his tickets and collected $300,000 in ticket sales, he would only need to raise $100,000 to book the venue and launch his marketing campaign.

To plug that $100,000 hole, the entrepreneur went to his friends and family. They had their doubts, but he was able to raise the money. He invested heavily in event marketing and, just a few months later, ticket sales opened with 40 percent sold on the first day. He did it! Well, he thought he did.

For his customers to pay by credit card, the entrepreneur had to open a merchant account, which is a special type of account allowing the entrepreneur's business to accept certain types of payment. Due to how common fraud is in the events industry and the high risk of chargebacks if an event held by a new company is cancelled, merchant account companies are wary of immediately releasing funds to events companies with a limited operating history. When the merchant account provider saw all the money from the ticket sales rolling in, it quickly froze most of the funds and refused to release them until the event was held.

The entrepreneur panicked and went rushing back to his friends and family for the needed $300,000. Sadly, but unsurprisingly, he found them angry and unable to provide more funding. With the event just a few months away, the entrepreneur scrambled and began looking for last-minute investors. Unceremoniously, his key suppliers were already demanding their deposits to commit to the event, and when they weren't paid, they began dropping out. With the company in a full-blown cash crisis and major event features being cancelled, refunds for ticket purchases began rolling in and the event collapsed. The initial $100,000 investment went up in smoke. This all could have been avoided with a detailed financial model that meticulously worked through the assumptions and logistical details contained in the terms and conditions of his supplier agreements (including his merchant account provider).

**Sample Use of Proceeds for
Media and Entertainment Company–Next 12 Months**

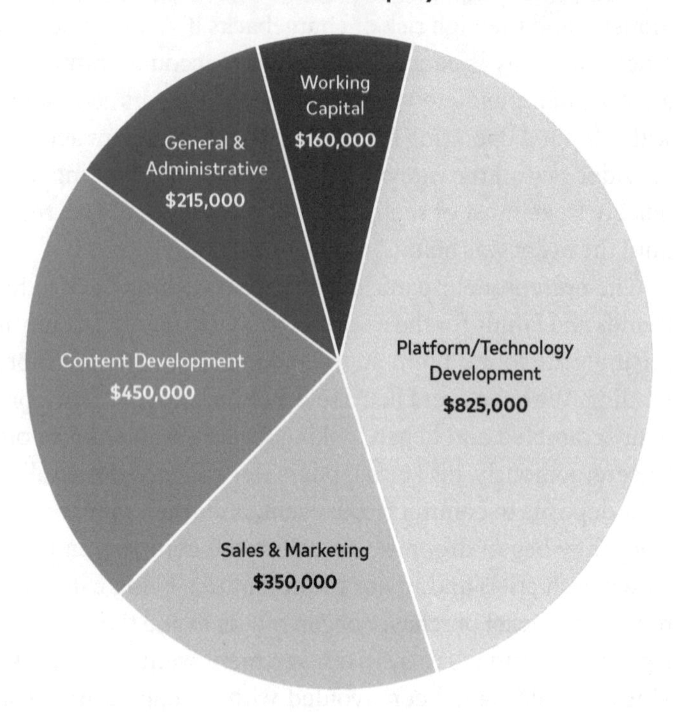

Platform/Technology Development	$825,000
Sales & Marketing	$350,000
Content Development	$450,000
General & Administrative	$215,000
Working Capital	$160,000
Total Use of Proceeds	**$2,000,000**

12

Understand Your Key Performance Indicators (KPIS)

IT WILL be a challenge to develop your business successfully without your team having a quantified understanding of your company's operating and financial circumstances, including how they scale (i.e., change as you grow). We'd like you to face challenges head-on, so they don't rear their heads at the wrong time, like during an investor pitch.

You must be intimately familiar with the suite of metrics most relevant to and revealing of your company's performance. How else will you know how you're doing? More importantly, for the purpose of raising money, how will you communicate to investors how well you are doing? You need to know your business, including its numbers, better than anyone to convince people that there is real and achievable value in what you're selling.

Persuasion is accomplished with thoughtful and satisfactory answers to an investor's questions. It's your business, so investors expect you to know what metrics are most important to assessing your company's performance—we describe some metrics later in this chapter. If you want an investor to trust you with their money, you must show them you care about the same things they do, so talk numbers like a person who is paying attention and knows what her customer acquisition cost is. If you don't, you're hurting the chances that you raise money. In fact, it has been said that in their pitch, not knowing their numbers is where most entrepreneurs stumble.

To alleviate investors' concerns, you want to demonstrate an adept handling of the metrics relevant to companies that operate in your industry. For example, if you are pitching an investor on a new social media platform, be familiar with the concept of Monthly Active Users (MAUs), how the big industry players measure it, and how it relates to your performance.

When Twitter went public with its S-1 (the document a company files when first listing its securities on a public stock exchange in the United States), it explained that MAUs are a measure of the size of its active user base. Twitter defined MAUs as users who logged in and accessed Twitter through its website, mobile website, desktop or mobile applications, SMS, or registered third-party applications or websites in the thirty-day period ending on the date of measurement. The company further explained that average MAUs for a period represents the average of the MAUs at the end of each month during the period. Finally, Twitter provided year-over-year growth comparisons for three-month periods in the United States and the rest of the world. Of course, these metrics don't provide perfect insights. Elon Musk's acquisition of Twitter brought to the forefront the debate over how many of the company's users were merely bots pumping out spam.

Simply put, knowing your numbers is essential for entrepreneurs who want to raise capital. This knowledge shows you understand you're running a business, not dabbling in a passion project. Don't let something you can control be the reason you fail to get funding.

Why do investors care so much about performance metrics and your knowledge of them? We would lump everything under two overarching reasons: (1) metrics offer an objective assessment of performance, and (2) managerial focus on producing and analyzing performance metrics demonstrates an understanding of value creation. Translation: KPIs show that management and investors are focused on the same thing—making money and understanding how their business does (or doesn't do) that.

If you don't know your numbers, you can't have a clear view of your profit potential and the path to it. If you can't see this path, it's worth considering whether your idea is better suited to a not-for-profit or a charity. It could still be a great idea, but securing funds for such a pursuit requires different things than for a start-up with high-growth potential. Consider whether there is a viable path to profit before you hit the streets.

Regularly reviewing your company's KPIs will also help you identify problems with your business. You can't fix what you don't know is broken. Put in some time to run and study your numbers to maximize the chances of a successful raise. Here's an example of a hypothetical conversation you don't want to have:

Investor: What are your customer acquisition cost, customer churn rate, and lifetime value metrics? We need to understand your customer acquisition strategies and whether they scale.

Entrepreneur: We're in a growing market, so it's hard to pin those figures down.

Investor: If you don't have reasoned estimates, how are you so confident this will be a profitable venture?

Entrepreneur: Well, it's a great idea, isn't it?

Investor: Maybe, but if you can't tell me your customer acquisition cost and the scalability of the acquisition strategy it supports, then how do I know whether your business gains economic value by scaling?

Entrepreneur: Let me investigate it and I'll get back to you.

Meeting ends.

Investors need to trust you before they hand over their money. You're a total stranger who is not relevant in their life beyond this interaction from which you are hoping to gain. You build trust by demonstrating value to investors through competence.

If you're building a start-up, you must know the operational and financial metrics investors care about and what they represent, or at least have someone on your team available who does know and can speak to them. If you stumble on the numbers in the first few pitches, you may still be successful, but it will take longer and could poison the well. If you are properly prepared from the get-go, it's more likely you will avoid eliminating wanted investors as options.

On that note, let's talk about some of these metrics you must understand to successfully line the company coffers.

Economically Acquiring Customers and Scaling

Arguably the most important thing to understand about metrics is the relationship between customer acquisition cost (CAC) and lifetime value per customer (LTV).

It's difficult to overemphasize how important understanding your business through these metrics is and how necessary it is to have efficient systems in place to collect, analyze, and interpret the data needed for these calculations to impress potential investors and successfully raise money. If you are asked how much it costs you to acquire customers, vague meandering answers citing "marketing efforts" will not do. If you're betting the farm on "viral growth," you'll probably be making that bet alone.

Customer Acquisition Cost

Customer acquisition cost is essentially how much you spend acquiring customers divided by the number of customers acquired over some period. How much you spend acquiring customers is made up of your sales and marketing costs. Yes, this includes salaries and any costs that vary based on the number of personnel, such as licensing fees for marketing software. Divide this aggregate cost by customer volume to calculate CAC on a per-customer basis.

You can analyze individual tools you're using as part of your customer acquisition strategy. For example, analyze how much you're spending on certain search engines or other sites to generate customer leads and the volume of customers being converted from each provider. If some providers are providing significantly better "customer acquisition" returns than others, you will likely want to reshuffle how you're approaching customer acquisition.

Don't let this quick summary belie the intensive analysis that understanding your CAC requires. You'll need a detailed breakdown of the costs involved in generating sales, the lead times required to acquire those customers, how much is spent on a customer before they are monetized, and a whole host of other variables. We highly recommend further reading (see the resource pages) and speaking to an advisor. If you can demonstrate a sophisticated understanding of your business from this perspective, you're starting off on the right foot.

Lifetime Value

Lifetime value per customer is the value you get from a customer so long as they remain one. In other words, LTV represents your company's ability to get money from its customers. You can calculate LTV on a gross or net basis. Meaning, you can measure it from a total revenue perspective or from a contribution margin perspective (i.e., money left over once you pay incremental variable costs associated with the sale and any installation, support, and service costs expected over the customer's lifetime).

In a formula, LTV calculated on a net basis equals annual customer contribution margin *multiplied by* average customer lifespan (in years). If you want to calculate this figure on a gross basis, just swap out "customer contribution margin" for "customer revenue."

LTV to CAC Ratio

The astute among you will recognize that, if LTV is not greater than CAC over the long run, your company doesn't have a viable business plan—it will lose money. You can't make money if it costs you more to acquire customers than the amount you receive from those customers.

At a bare minimum, your LTV / CAC ratio should be greater than 1 (or you should have a clear and reasonable path to that destination). To attract investors, LTV will have to be larger than CAC by an amount sufficient to generate investors' required return.

Investors will also consider how long it will take for LTV to outpace CAC. If it's going to take twenty years, they probably won't be interested.

Scaling the Customer Acquisition Model

If you've shown investors that you've got an economically viable business model (i.e., your LTV / CAC ratio is greater than 1), they'll want to know if your model can predictably scale. This determination will be driven by the extent to which your customer acquisition model is predictable or a black hole. If an investor can't predict with some certainty, or using some historically justified basis, how your CAC and the ratio between your CAC and LTV will evolve as you scale up, how will they know if your company is a worthwhile investment? Be ready to discuss this.

Other Practical Metrics

To leave you with a few other practical metrics to consider, and ways of thinking to adopt, let's take a brief look at some relevant metrics in the social media and flexible workspace solutions spaces. If you're working on a business in a different industry, then find a comparable company and pull their annual return (10-K) and prospectus (S-1) (or the Canadian equivalents) and see what they have to say about key performance metrics. Many metrics reflect the same figures the founders and other executives would have discussed with investors when they were pitching the business for funding in rounds before going public.

Social Media Metrics (Twitter)

Returning to our Twitter example, the company cares about more than just MAUs. When marketing its securities to the public for the first time, it provided details about:

- **Timeline views.** Used to measure engagement, timeline views are the total number of timelines requested when registered users visit Twitter, refresh a timeline, or view search results while logged in.

- **Timeline views per MAU.** Also used to measure engagement, this metric is calculated by dividing the total timeline views for a period by the average MAUs for the last three months of the period.
- **Advertising revenue per timeline view.** Used as a measure of the company's ability to monetize its platform, this metric represents advertising revenue per 1,000 timeline views during an applicable period.
- **User engagement.** User engagement is measured by timeline views and the number of timeline views per MAU, all of which are assessed by platform (mobile, desktop, etc.).
- **Monetization.** Monetization measures the revenue the company generates through advertising per timeline view.

As you can see, these metrics will help inform Twitter's board and executive team about how well changes in corporate actions are affecting the company's revenue generation and overall user engagement; this information becomes particularly useful when tracked over time.

Flexible Workspace Solutions (WeWork)

WeWork's storied initial public offering (IPO) may have been taxing for many, as the company's valuation tumbled to just a fraction of the original expectations set close to the $50 billion mark, but today it is still a multibillion-dollar business that went public via a special purpose acquisition vehicle. WeWork focused on describing the following:

- **Workstation capacity.** The estimated number of workstations available at open WeWork locations. This metric provides an indication of how many more customers WeWork can service and potential incremental revenue generation opportunities. In particular, it indicates the ability to sell memberships across the company's global platform.
- **Memberships.** The cumulative number of WeWork memberships (providing workstation access from standard solutions and configurations) and on-demand memberships (providing access to shared workstations or private spaces as needed, by the minute, by the hour, or by the day). Standard and on-demand membership types are both counted as one membership. Memberships are a key indicator of adoption of the company's global platform, the scale and reach of its network, and its ability to fill locations with members.
- **Enterprise membership percentage.** Memberships attributable to enterprise members, which are organizations with five hundred or more full-time employees, as a percentage of total memberships. Enterprise members are not required to have any minimum number of workstations attributable to them. They are important to the company because these memberships are typically longer-term commitments for multiple solutions across the company's global platform.
- **Run-rate revenue.** For a given period, revenue for the last month of the period multiplied by twelve. This metric is used to measure the magnitude of the company's scale at a given point in time.
- **Committed revenue backlog.** As of a given date, total non-cancelable contractual commitments, net of discounts,

remaining under agreements entered as of that date, which the company expects to be recognized as revenue after such date. Committed backlog provides insight into WeWork's future performance and indicates the level of sustained demand for its solutions and the degree of revenue predictability in its business.

13

Look for Cheap Early Money

THE INVESTORS willing to accept the enormous risk accompanying bets on new companies, new ideas, and even new management teams have certain expectations for the return they will make on their investment. That expectation is, in two words, "a lot."

This means early-stage capital tends to be very expensive for founders (often in the form of dilution), especially if their business is in its initial stages and doesn't have much to show. Investors typically want a bigger chunk of your company if you have not developed a prototype, because it's a bigger risk than if you have a working product with big lead orders.

When capital costs are high, seek lower-cost alternatives. This raises the question: What are those lower-cost alternatives? Who is willing to put money into a high-risk entrepreneur without seeking out the same kinds of demanding returns reasonable investors require?

Enter the Government

Regardless of where you live in the world, governments tend to be keen on entrepreneurship, or at least say they are. Some do little more than offer a few words of encouragement, but many have developed an extensive array of programs and institutions specifically tasked with helping entrepreneurs launch their ideas and grow.

Government support can come in the form of soft assistance, such as hosting a networking forum, but it can also come in the form of cold hard cash. This capital may be structured as a loan, such as a U.S. Small Business Administration microloan (sometimes at a below-market rate). It can also come in the form of a grant, such as a grant for tech start-ups from the Small Business Innovation Research program in the U.S. or the NRC Industrial Research Assistance Program in Canada. With grants, generally a company does not need to give any equity to the government or repay the amount received. Grant money can seem like "free money" since you don't need to repay it. However, bear in mind that applying for grants is a lengthy task. Even just identifying applicable grants can be a taxing endeavor.

While governments can be big suppliers of entrepreneurial support, other institutions, companies, and funds have been known to provide support to entrepreneurs, too. So now that you know programs are willing to dole out cash to your business, what should you do about it?

Grant and Competition Landscaping

Every company should landscape (i.e., look for) opportunities for inexpensive capital. The two types of landscaping to conduct are grant landscaping and competition landscaping.

Grant landscaping is the process of searching for and identifying grants your company can qualify for and potentially win. Depending on your industry, the life cycle stage of your company, and other unique factors such as the diversity of your management team, you may find your business qualifies for a sizable number of grants from various public and private institutions.

Once you have identified these grants, you will realize applying for and winning grants is not a simple process. Grant applications can take an inordinate amount of time to prepare and will likely require extensive details about your company's financials, operations, management team, and plans.

It is not uncommon for some companies that qualify for many grants to engage a full-time grant writer just to prepare applications. If you are going down this road, we recommend hiring a professional grant writer or an English major—most can be punchy when they need to, and God knows they need the money.

The second type of landscaping to undertake is competition landscaping. Despite the name, it has nothing to do with spying on your competitors. Rather, competition landscaping is the process of identifying pitch competitions to take part in that can provide considerable awards and exposure. Some of these competitions include America's Seed Fund (U.S.), the Startup World Cup (global), and Inventures Startup Pitch (Canada).

Many institutions—including consultancies, banks, accelerators, incubators, and investment funds—host competitions where entrepreneurs pitch their business in hopes of winning a prize. The prizes from these competitions can include mentorship opportunities, access to professional services, and in select cases, cash. Even if you do not win one these competitions, they are a great way to meet professionals, introduce your product or service to potential customers, and refine your pitch.

These competitions are not a free lunch, though; they take a lot of time and resources to prepare for. But the benefits of participation can be staggering. We know one young CEO who raised more than $250,000 for her business purely from participating in pitch competitions.

Grant and competition landscaping should be considered essential for any early-stage company. Don't think of stopping just because you closed another round of financing. As your business matures and changes, your company may qualify for other grants and competitions. That's good for you because every dollar reduces ultimate dilution.

Not All "Cheap" Money Is Inexpensive

When pursuing inexpensive capital, be wary! Not all sources branding themselves as inexpensive or founder-friendly are. Some institutions may offer you "mentorship" or office space, but in exchange will demand a considerable share of your company. It might feel like you are getting a good deal when you are starting out, but as your business matures, you could be stunned to see just how much you gave away. Regardless of the type or amount of funding you receive, always read the fine print and fully understand the expectations and obligations of your business.

Validation

In the end, the more grants and inexpensive capital you can get, the better your prospects are of securing external financing and the less dilutive that financing will be. These funds will allow you to advance your business before meeting with an investor, which creates an opportunity to present a more well-developed product and secure better economic terms for your company. The process of grant writing and competing will also force you to articulate your company goals, chart out how to achieve them, and reflect on your business plan. All these outcomes should translate into a better pitch and heightened ability to field investors' questions.

Finally, there is a powerful affirmation effect from receiving funding from these sources. If you manage to collect a considerable sum from grants, competitions, or other similar means, it will make a good impression on investors. The fact that you competed with other entrepreneurs and won sends a strong signal that you have an excellent concept endorsed by others. By no means will these victories guarantee investor funding, but they will strengthen your case for it.

For more information on some of the grants and competitions available to entrepreneurs, check out our resource pages.

14

Plan for Taxes Today

IT SHOULD be no surprise that not all companies are treated equally by all levels of government.

Politicians and bureaucrats have a long history of incentivizing certain economic behaviors and specific interests by using alluring tax incentives. Sometimes those same politicians and bureaucrats discourage other behaviors by slapping select products, services, and companies with tax disincentives. (Just because some economic activity is attached to a tax incentive or disincentive, it does not necessarily mean that activity is useful for or harmful to society.)

Entrepreneurs raising capital understandably tend to shuffle tax planning to the bottom of their to-do list. After all, they have countless other things commanding their attention. From developing a customer-engagement strategy, to launching products, to sourcing suppliers, there is no shortage of tasks. Entrepreneurs may think of taxes as a matter to address once they are profitable and a successful exit is reasonably foreseeable. And if you don't expect to be profitable for several years while your business ramps up, allocating time to tax planning can feel like a waste. Regardless of the reason, putting off tax planning may cost you later. The right approach, as with most things, is to plan ahead.

Depending on what industry you are in, you might find that you will owe taxes before you are even profitable. Crazy, right? More importantly, your company's tax treatment will significantly influence your overall profitability, your ability to generate returns for your shareholders, and how much cash you need to ask for in the first place. Understanding your company's tax treatment and any unique aspects of it is the smart way to approach a raise. We are not suggesting that you need to become an accountant, but you owe it to yourself to understand generally how taxes will affect your business—for better or worse.

Tax Treatments

Governments offer tax incentives to companies for many reasons. They might offer them based on who the company hires, where it operates, its industry, the technology it is developing, how much it exports, how high its revenue is, and, in very rare cases, other less-above-board reasons we've all seen portrayed in steamy dramas. A classic example of an industry with a broadly favorable tax treatment is film. Industry participants are often given tax breaks with the justification that shooting a production in a certain location can boost the local economy.

Generally, these tax incentives develop when the government wants the market to undertake a certain activity to achieve some purpose. This activity may be hiring certain people, like veterans, or engaging in certain activities, such as the research and development of intellectual property related to green energy. These incentives can assume a variety of forms. Since this is not a tax textbook, we will stick to a handful of basic concepts that can come into play with young companies.

- **Tax rebate.** With a tax rebate, governments will send you money to refund certain expenses. Rebates can be common with payroll expenses, where governments may offer to repay you for a percentage of an employee's wages.
- **Tax credit.** There are multiple types of tax credits, but the basic premise is that tax credits can be used to lower your tax bill. Companies can apply tax credits they qualify for to lower the amount of taxes they owe, or in some cases, to collect a direct cash refund. Seen another way, tax credits are masked government spending, as the government foregoes collecting taxes owed to it.
- **Lower nominal tax rates.** While the nominal corporate income tax rate in a jurisdiction might be 26.5 percent, a government may offer a lower overall rate depending on a company's size or industry. For example, many governments offer small-business tax rates, where companies earning less than a certain amount of profit pay a lower corporate income tax rate than companies earning above that threshold.
- **Tax holiday.** In some cases, entrepreneurs are given a tax holiday (meaning they are not required to pay select taxes they would otherwise have to pay, such as property taxes). Tax holidays are common in economically devastated areas where local governments are trying to spur development by offering entrepreneurs tax relief to locate there. Can't get blood from a stone, after all.

Altogether, the economic benefits of tapping all available tax incentives can profoundly affect a company (and a founder's realized wealth when they sell their company). For a list of common tax advantages for entrepreneurs, check out the resource pages at the end of this book.

Lest you think tax treatments are all good news for companies, we must warn you that on occasion they can cut the other way. A common example is an excise tax, which is an additional tax imposed on the manufacture or sale of a particular good or service. Governments can have a variety of reasons for implementing excise taxes, such as to promote public health or to help the environment. Regardless of the policy rationale, the net effect is that consumers pay more. In many countries, these taxes are particularly common on the sale of alcohol, tobacco, and fuel.

While excise taxes generally apply to a narrow range of products, they can be enormously impactful if your company is manufacturing one of those products. For example, if you and your friends were thinking of launching your own micro-brewery or winery, you would need to understand the timing, nature, and value of excise taxes you will be responsible for paying and how your cash flow planning is affected. This knowledge affects your pricing strategy, as you need to recoup the tax amount from your consumers. It also impacts the sales volume you need to break even and start earning a profit.

Regardless of whether a tax benefit helps or hurts you, keep in mind that these tax treatments usually carry administrative costs and headaches. Payroll rebate programs, such as those for scientific research, can require extensive documentation to prove the funds are being spent on qualifying activities. Depending on the state of your operation, this might add material accounting costs to your business. The broader point is, think downstream about the knock-on effects of each choice you make.

Ignorance Is No Excuse

Ignorance of your company's unique tax treatment can significantly affect your ability to raise money. If you identify material tax benefits, you might realize you need far less capital and can provide your investor with an even better potential return than you originally thought (while lessening your dilution)—all things that can help smooth the fundraising process. Conversely, missing out on material tax factors can make the process harder than it needs to be, and increases the risk of being embarrassed when an investor asks about them.

Speaking with other entrepreneurs in your industry and searching government websites for available tax benefits based on your company's business activities is an excellent starting point. After this preliminary research, getting advice from a tax professional who specializes in your industry is a valuable next step. You will need a tax accountant anyway if you get your business past the ideation phase. Asking potential candidates to help you understand your business's tax environment poses an excellent opportunity to test their value-add for your industry and their ability to communicate with you. You can always go straight to the tax professional and skip the personal research, but if you are interested in saving money, you can do a little homework first.

Blown Raise Story: An American Pipe Dream

An American entrepreneur was looking to capitalize when his home state legalized cannabis for both medical and recreational use. Cannabis was still illegal at the federal level in the United States, but his state announced it would be licensing cannabis companies to operate in a similar fashion as other states that had previously legalized cannabis. The entrepreneur put together a business case for a cultivation facility and dispensary and was able to book a pitch meeting with a cannabis investment group that had invested in other states and was eyeing this new jurisdiction for investment.

While the entrepreneur was showing investors his financial projections, one of the fund managers squinted at the document and asked the entrepreneur about his "280e strategy" and why he could not see the impact on the entrepreneur's projections. The entrepreneur was extremely confused and asked the investor, "What is 280e?" The investor rolled his eyes and explained that because of cannabis's illegal status at the federal level, cannabis companies have an extremely punitive tax treatment. This treatment, colloquially referred to as 280e (with reference to the U.S. tax code), dramatically increases the effective tax rate of cannabis companies because it prevents them from deducting most ordinary business expenses (ouch!).

This tax treatment can result in large tax bills even if the business is unprofitable. Because the entrepreneur had not considered this tax effect, he would clearly require far more money than he was asking for. Obviously, the investor was concerned that the entrepreneur wasn't aware of such an elementary aspect of his business's tax framework and wondered what else the entrepreneur may have missed. The investor promptly passed on the deal.

15

Share the Wealth

IF YOU aspire to build a business of real scale, it has probably dawned on you that you will not be doing it alone. You will need a team whose members not only possess the skills required to construct your vision but are also willing to assume the considerable risk associated with joining a nascent company. To assemble this team, you need a compelling case that your company is a place people want to be.

Prospective key hires won over by your vision will quickly inquire about compensation, including what ownership interest they will receive. After all, you have told them they are instrumental to how you plan on building a great business. Why wouldn't they expect a piece of the profits? We don't want your first inclination to be to stall or tell the prospective hires not to get ahead of themselves.

If you have no plan to appropriately compensate your future colleagues for the considerable risk they are assuming by joining you, do not be surprised if they do not return your calls. Lots of founders see the value in sharing the (potential) wealth; those who don't are hampering themselves in a significant way.

Team Alignment

An essential quality of any entrepreneurial team is alignment between the company's success and the team's success. Obviously, the company's success is a positive thing for the team, as it means salaries will continue being paid, but the people who willingly joined you early on are not in it only for their salaries.

Younger companies, which are routinely cash constrained as they try to grow, tend to pay salaries and offer benefits less attractive than what a more mature company would offer, while also often demanding more of their employees. If your key employees do not have an ownership stake and are working only for a lower cash salary than they could get somewhere else, it's doubtful they will go the extra mile to help your company succeed. Few employees may be willing to risk their reputation by vouching to an investor that your company is a worthwhile bet if they have no upside besides a sub-par paycheck. If you really believe your colleagues are a critical and indispensable part of your company's future success, then they should be compensated as such.

A major risk of not effectively aligning your employees' financial success with that of the company is that these employees may be perpetually more likely to have wandering eyes as they look for a new job. They may even decide company time is the best time to look for one! Making matters worse, they may join one of your competitors, especially if the founders include equity as part of the compensation package.

By the way, if you think that "non-compete" agreement you made your employees sign will stop them from working for one of your competitors, don't be so sure. The ability to enforce a non-compete clause varies tremendously based on where your company operates, where the employee works, and the type of role covered. Regardless of what your employees agreed to in their employment agreements, you may find the non-compete section is simply unenforceable.

The ESOP

Founders who recognize the need to regularly enlarge their team as they grow will have the good sense to implement a mechanism to readily issue ownership to new team members as they join the company. Early-stage companies are routinely absorbing new talent, so they commonly set up an employee stock ownership plan, colloquially known as an ESOP. An ESOP, pronounced ee-sop, essentially creates a pool of potential ownership that can be distributed to employees as needed, as approved by the board.

The size of the ESOP pool varies based on the size of the company, the riskiness of the business, and the demands of external investors. For more mature companies, a pool of just 10 percent of the company's total ownership is relatively common, while for younger and riskier companies, this pool might be as large as 15 to 20 percent. If a company is particularly cash poor and the opportunity presents an exceptional degree of risk, it might even exceed 20 percent to bring in talent.

ESOPs are useful not only for incentivizing new employees, but also for distributing additional ownership stakes to existing employees and founders who have stood out for their contributions and quality of work. External investors in your company will likely take a leading role in determining the size of your ESOP, to ensure it is large enough to incentivize and attract the necessary people. Meaning, they'll decide whether for your business you should be closer to the 10 percent or 20 percent end of the spectrum. Ensuring your team is sufficiently motivated is something investors take seriously. If you have not done so effectively, they may require changes in this area as a condition of their investment.

Investor Redistribution Risk

Some founders manage to entice teams to work for them despite offering very little, if any, equity. These founders may believe they have been particularly clever negotiators by convincing their colleagues to accept so little, but that does not mean their prospective investors will tolerate it.

Before writing a check, competent investors will examine your capitalization table, commonly referred to as a "cap table," which details your company's current owners and their ownership positions (see an example at the end of this chapter). The cap table is very important, as shown in the first season of *Silicon Valley* when investor Peter Gregory discovers he agreed to pay $200,000 for 5 percent of Pied Piper while Erlich Bachman (immortalized by T.J. Miller) owns 10 percent merely because he provided the show's innovator Richard Hendricks with a "futon." Carta is an example of a software service that can help companies maintain an organized and current cap table and record of employee stock option ownership (including associated valuations for tax purposes).

An obvious reason for this examination is to confirm that the investment terms and overall ownership percentage you offered them in your pitch syncs up with reality. A perhaps less obvious reason for this examination is so they can see the respective ownership of the company's founders and key employees to ensure their compensation is sufficient to keep them highly motivated.

You can understand why an investor would have cause for concern if your tech company's chief technology officer, who is developing the patents critical to your success, owns no interest in the company. Investors will be relying on you and your team to build your business, and the notion of key team members not having a significant stake in its future can be a very serious issue. Sometimes, as a condition of providing financing, investors force founders to redistribute a large chunk of their equity to other key employees.

A Warning on Taxes

If your company plans to compensate its team with ownership, you must speak to a tax professional before you start doling out equity. We know tax planning may not be top of mind before you have even made a profit or raised any money, but tax advice is necessary for any company planning to distribute equity incentives.

What's the risk of not speaking to a professional beforehand? You may inadvertently create a hefty tax bill for one of your employees, even if neither your company nor the employee has the cash to pay it. People talk, so how is it going to look to prospective employees you'll need to tap as you grow if you inadvertently created a large cash bill payable to the government for other hires? Every government has its own approach to taxing equity incentives. If you do not consider this before writing up your incentive plan, your government may decide a key employee owes them tax dollars for equity that employee received, even if they have no means to convert that position into cash. This is an ugly situation you want to avoid.

NEW VENTURE COMPANY: SIMPLIFIED CAPITALIZATION TABLE

Holder	Series A Preferred Shares (#)	Common Shares (#)	Pro Rata Common Ownership Assuming Conversion and Full Allocation of Unallocated Options (%)*
Founders/Management			
Michael Miller		5,000,000	32.47%
Alexander Baker		5,000,000	32.47%
Investors			
John Miller		500,000	3.25%
Lisa Baker		400,000	2.60%
Venture Fund L.P.	3,000,000		19.48%
Employee Stock Option Pool			
Granted Options		500,000	3.25%
Unallocated Options		1,000,000	6.49%
Totals	3,000,000	12,400,000	100.00%

*Assumes Series A Preferred Shares convert to common at a 1:1 ratio.

16

People Will Leave

WE HAVE made it abundantly clear that it is essential to align the founders' and key employees' interests with the business by providing them a chance to share in the company's future success. Having a plan to provide them with equity as a motivator is a great start, but it is only that. You also need to plan for what happens if things don't work out. In essence, the founders and key employees need a prenuptial agreement with the company.

No matter how well you know someone, how smart they are, or how much they have accomplished, how they will perform in a start-up is unknown until you have seen them in action. Start-ups are fast-moving environments where everyone learns as they go. Leaders run into roadblocks at every turn. Many otherwise talented people simply aren't cut out for it. Founders and first hires may be geared up and excited to be part of something new at the outset, but they can lose interest quickly (especially when things get tough) and leave to focus on things more important to them (family, job security, travel, another start-up, etc.).

This presents a challenge to founders who want to ensure key people are motivated but also need to manage the risk that these people might quit in short order and take their equity with them. It can kill a company's ability to succeed if a founder or key employee can quit whenever and walk away with a sizable slice of the company while leaving their former peers behind to do the hard work. It is also a situation that prospective investors will find extremely unpalatable.

For several reasons, investors in emerging companies do not want to see a significant ownership stake held by anyone who is not working at the company or who didn't pay for it in an earlier round. First, it signals poor planning. Second, it creates a need to replace those who left with new personnel who will likely also need to be given equity to ensure proper motivation. This is called unnecessary issuance (distributing equity to two people for the same role instead of one), leaving less equity for those who actually stick around. Finally, investors who put up their own cash will not be keen to share any decision-making power with long-gone personnel whose presence in the company was transient.

So, how does a founder avoid this problem?

Set Clear Expectations among Founders and Early Executives

It is important that, before you go out to raise your first round, you and your team recognize the possibility that one of you might leave and plan accordingly. It is great you all came up with an idea together and are itching to get going, but that doesn't mean you will all be entitled to share equally in the company's fortune if one of you decides to abandon ship or starts working against the company's interests. If you don't have this conversation *before* you start meeting with investors, you may find one of you absolutely opposing any form of vesting, perhaps at a critical juncture in your negotiation, and it could scuttle your raise. People can change when (potential) money is involved.

Vesting

A common approach start-ups have adopted to tackle the issue of founders and key employees absconding with their shares (or options to purchase shares) before accomplishing much is through a concept called "vesting." Vesting means that an individual employee's or founder's allocated equity isn't truly theirs until certain conditions are satisfied. If someone's shares have not vested, it generally means they don't own those shares and are not entitled to the rights associated with them (voting rights, dividend rights, etc.). As it relates to options, a holder will have no right to exercise those options until they are vested (and subject to any other limitation on exercise as well).

How an individual's shares vest and become theirs depends on the methodology chosen by the company. Time-based vesting, as the name implies, is a method where shares vest by the passage of time (assuming continued employment). Alternatively, vesting can be linked to the achievement of certain corporate performance goals or individual milestones. This is known as performance-based vesting or milestone-based vesting (sometimes the two are combined). The written schedule of these timing and performance details is called a vesting schedule. Investors will review these schedules during their due diligence process.

Time-Based Vesting

Time-based vesting can be done a few different ways. It is common for entrepreneurs to employ "cliffs" when designing time-vesting schedules for their companies. With cliff vesting, the first portion of an individual's equity vests at a fixed date. For example, you could have a one-year cliff where 100 percent of an employee's equity vests after their first year of service. In this scenario, someone who lasted only six weeks on the job and discovered it wasn't for them won't take any equity when they head for the door, but after the one-year mark hits, they will.

Alternatively, partial cliffs can be used. These are set up so only a portion of an employee's equity vests upon a fixed date, while the rest vests gradually at shorter specified intervals over time. For example, a vesting schedule may be set up so the first 50 percent of an equity award vests after one year of employment, with the remaining 50 percent gradually vesting over the next few years—perhaps at 2 percent per month for the next twenty-five months. This gradual vesting over time is known as graded vesting, and its use can provide a continuing stream of commitment over time once an initial cliff has been cleared.

Performance- or Milestone-Based Vesting

Performance-based or milestone-based vesting plans can be customized in many ways. They can be tied to generating sales leads, filing patents, or launching a new product by a specific deadline—whatever the board desires. While this considerable flexibility may seem attractive, be very cautious about using performance-based vesting when your company is in its infancy.

The milestones you set when your company is first coming together may seem appropriate, but this could change radically as product development plans change or unexpected financial obligations arise. An individual whose equity is tied to sales generated from a new product will quickly become frustrated and demoralized if that product is delayed or needs to be reworked.

You might also inadvertently poison the well among your team if everyone has different milestones and some are readily achieved while others are not (or are sidelined altogether). Perceived fairness (whether someone had "easier" targets than another) can quickly cause infighting and demands for revision, which takes managerial time away from growing the business.

Reverse Vesting

When you and your co-founders start meeting investors, there is a good chance you will have already divided the initial company equity among yourselves and will own your stakes outright. Prepare yourselves for the possibility that an interested big check investor might want to put you and your fellow co-founders on a reverse vesting schedule.

Don't let the term trip you up. Reverse vesting is used when you already own your shares. It is a tool for external investors to ensure ongoing commitment. Reverse vesting provides companies the right to repurchase a declining number of your shares (usually for a nominal amount of money, so don't get excited) if certain things happen for a certain period of time. Like the other forms of vesting, reverse vesting is done according to a schedule that can be time-based, performance-based, or a combination of the two.

For a simple example, say you and your three co-founders collectively own 100 percent of your company and you each have 4 million shares. An investor might ask for a three-year time-based vesting schedule where 75 percent of your shares (3 million) can be repurchased by the company if you leave or are terminated for cause, but after every year of service completed, the company loses the right to purchase one-third of those 3 million shares (1 million). Eventually, after three years, they won't be able to purchase any of your shares if you leave. Alternatively, if you left the company a minute after the deal closed to "find yourself" and traverse the Andes, you would keep only 1 million shares, while the remaining 3 million would be purchased by the company for a nominal price (pennies on the dollar) or outright terminated.

Keep in mind that many investors out there, particularly angels investing in early rounds, may never ask to put you or your team on a reverse vesting schedule. Other investors managing large pools of capital may be more likely to demand it. Once their capital is committed, they do not want to be caught without a plan to deal with one of you leaving early.

A competent corporate lawyer can provide valuable insight on how to assemble vesting terms and equity awards documents aligning your team's interests with the company while assuaging investors' concerns about the future. They can also advise you to push back when an investor's reverse vesting demands on founders are too harsh and should be rejected outright.

Wait! What if...?

When told they will be subject to a vesting or reverse vesting schedule, many employees and founders start worrying about theoretical events that could prevent their shares from vesting. What if the company gets bought out before their shares are vested? Would they get nothing? Or what if the bigwigs cynically plan to fire you a day before a cliff so they can keep all the equity to themselves after you helped them land a bunch of big clients?

These are real concerns. These events *could* happen. Thankfully, these are concerns proper planning and documentation can address. We wish we could tell you there is some easy way to address them, but the reality is it does boil down to having the right language in the legal documents. We'll keep emphasizing it: hire competent professionals.

Equity awards containing vesting schedules may be accompanied by acceleration provisions that cause full vesting of an individual's equity upon certain events. For example, your shares might immediately vest if a strategic investor wants to buy out your company, allowing you to get paid out upon closing of the sale. Alternatively, some acceleration provisions will require that if the company is bought out, you need to ride out your vesting schedule working for the acquirer.

Of course, there is a risk that management over at the acquirer may decide to axe you once they close on the deal. (Your own management might even decide they don't need you before the deal closes.) To address these possible scenarios, acceleration provisions can accommodate for individual termination events. Depending on the reason for someone being terminated, their vesting terms may permit a portion, if not all, of their remaining unvested equity to vest. If the reason for termination, however, is that the individual was leaking secrets to competitors or stealing from the company, a well-written equity award will see that their unvested equity is forfeited.

Blown Raise Story: A Distracted Founder

Two long-time friends of over twenty-five years decided to launch a software venture. The two had very complementary skill sets. One was a fantastic operator and tech expert and the other had a finance and investing background centered on software.

The two founders went in with the understanding they would be equal partners. They evenly divided 90 percent of the company's equity among themselves and allocated 10 percent to a few junior associates they hired. On the backs of their reputations, they quickly raised $4 million from their personal networks and were off to the races.

The founder with the finance background was always interested in a variety of opportunities and sat on several corporate boards, which occupied much of his time. While he was still working on the software venture, more and more of his time became occupied with other matters, and within six months he was doing the bare minimum and contributing only a few comments during the odd weekly meeting. While the tech-savvy founder was frustrated, he had a long-time relationship with his friend and figured that as things picked up, his friend would refocus his time, so he stayed silent.

After a year of operations, the company had achieved mixed progress and needed to begin meeting with investors for a new fundraising round. The finance-focused founder indicated he was relatively busy and sent one of his junior finance associates in his place to attend investor meetings. After nearly every investor meeting, investors began asking why one of the key founders, who owned a huge chunk of the company and was also the finance expert, was not attending these meetings. They also started asking why an executive who seemed part-time at best had such a large piece of the company's equity. One investor expressed his displeasure by saying he was "unhappy with so much dead weight on the cap table." (This is never something you want to hear.)

A few investors indicated they would consider investing, but only if the executives were placed on a reverse vesting schedule where they would have to re-earn their equity over time. The finance founder refused to be put on a reverse vesting schedule or give up any of his equity and said that they should just meet with "better investors." Unfortunately, at this point the other founder had no legal avenue to do anything about his intransigent co-founder, and after three months of repeated failures and this founder refusing to budge on his ownership, the company ran out of cash and flamed out. The friendship didn't last either.

Scenario A: Vesting Schedule for New Employees

- Venture Co. hired three new key employees
- These employees were granted 30,000 stock options each
- 50% of their stock options vested after their first year of service; 25% after their second year; and the last 25% after their third year
- One employee stayed past the end of their third year (Employee #1)
- One employee quit after year two and forfeited 25% of their options (Employee #2)
- One employee quit before completing year one and forfeited all their options (Employee #3)
- The forfeited options were returned to the company, which could reallocate them to other new hires

Scenario B: Reverse Vesting for Founders

- Two co-founders secured a $5M investment from a venture capital fund
- As a condition of the investment, the venture fund required both founders to accept a reverse vesting schedule for the next four years
- Reverse Vesting Terms: 80% of a founder's shares would be subject to repurchase by the company for a negligible amount if that founder quit
- After each year, the company would lose the conditional right to repurchase 20% of each founder's original share total (or one-quarter of each founder's shares that were subject to reverse vesting)

SCENARIO A: VESTING SCHEDULE FOR NEW HIRES

	Year 1	Year 2	Year 3	Total (Where Applicable)
Employee #1				
Total Unvested Options at Beginning of Year	30,000	15,000	7,500	
Options Vested in Year Based on Original Vesting Schedule	15,000	7,500	7,500	
Employment Status at Year End	Employed	Employed	Employed	
Options Vested in Year	15,000	7,500	7,500	30,000
Options Forfeited in Year	–	–	–	–
Employee #2				
Total Unvested Options at Beginning of Year	30,000	15,000	7,500	
Options Vested in Year Based on Original Vesting Schedule	15,000	7,500	7,500	
Employment Status at Year End	Employed	Employed	Not Employed (Quit)	
Options Vested in Year	15,000	7,500	–	22,500
Options Forfeited in Year	–	–	7,500	7,500
Employee #3				
Total Unvested Options at Beginning of Year	30,000	15,000	7,500	
Options Vested in Year Based on Original Vesting Schedule	15,000	7,500	7,500	
Employment Status at Year End	Not Employed (Quit)	Not Employed	Not Employed	
Options Vested in Year	–	–	–	–
Options Forfeited in Year	30,000	–	–	30,000
Total Options Forfeited by All Employees	30,000	–	7,500	37,500

SCENARIO B: REVERSE VESTING SCHEDULE FOR FOUNDERS

	Closing of Financing Round	End of Year 1	End of Year 2	End of Year 3	End of Year 4
Founder #1					
Total Common Shares	2,000,000	2,000,000	2,000,000	2,000,000	2,000,000
Common Shares Subject to Conditional Repurchase	1,600,000	1,200,000	800,000	400,000	-
Shares Not Subject to Conditional Repurchase	400,000	800,000	1,200,000	1,600,000	2,000,000
Founder #2					
Total Common Shares	3,000,000	3,000,000	3,000,000	3,000,000	3,000,000
Common Shares Subject to Conditional Repurchase	2,400,000	1,800,000	1,200,000	600,000	-
Shares Not Subject to Conditional Repurchase	600,000	1,200,000	1,800,000	2,400,000	3,000,000

In stage two, on preparing for the raise, we hope you gained insights on the importance of honest disclosure; organization; building a balanced, incentivized, and cohesive management team; preparing a data room, pitch deck, and financial model; understanding your key metrics; and getting the necessary professional advice. All these factors are important to consider as you get ready to present your business to investors. If you've done the work preparing your materials and practicing your pitch, you should be well on your way to ensuring that your pitch performance isn't a hinderance to closing your company's raise.

STAGE THREE

THE RAISE

YOUR TEAM is assembled, your pitch materials are prepared, you have researched your market and you understand it, and you know your numbers. You are ready to pitch investors. As an entrepreneur, you know individual investors and funds have seen hundreds, if not thousands, of other opportunities, and it is vital for you to stand out. After all, when raising money, you're selling a product; it just happens to be a financial product (financial securities).

At first contact, entrepreneurs must have the knowledge to effectively engage with investors. You also need to create a sense of trust that you and your team will professionally steward invested dollars. It is essential to speak an investor's language and understand their perspectives, especially when they condition their investment on certain terms. You want to align your interests with the investor's to get to closing, and you can't do that if you don't understand their perspective.

It's a small world, and investors share deep networks with other investors. Word can get around (bad travels faster), so it's best to present yourself professionally. To that end, make sure you show up prepared to make your pitch, whether you are given your full time allotment or only half of it. Be prepared to give a thirty-minute, fifteen-minute, five-minute, or thirty-second presentation. Arrive fifteen to twenty minutes early, and bring hard copies of your presentation in case there are technical difficulties. If your meeting will be a video call, clear your desktop and mind your background, ensure you have proper lighting, and consider getting a microphone so you're clearly audible.

Learning and understanding the early-stage finance markets and the various tangents related to them, while in the midst of a raise and running a business, presents a long and emotional roller coaster. Stage three offers a head start to understanding the experience and ways to avoid unforced errors so you can close the deal.

Time to discuss how to avoid "no" and get to "yes, I'll invest."

17

Be Confident, Not Cocky

DEMONSTRATING CONFIDENCE when presenting is critical to persuading your audience. There are many ways to demonstrate confidence, such as knowing your facts, speaking clearly and projecting, and answering questions directly. However, there is a fine line between demonstrating confidence and turning people off. You don't demonstrate confidence by telling people you are the best and that passing on this investment opportunity would be a mistake—but you knew that.

Instead, when making your pitch, demonstrate you're a human who recognizes that building great businesses requires a team (though one person can still be firmly in control). Communicate that you contribute your part of the work and take others' views seriously when doing so. And be mindful that different people respond positively to different approaches. Some gravitate to bravado while others prefer different personality styles. Do not expect that everyone will be captivated by yours.

Valuable time can be wasted on ego. This may happen at any organization with a culture of tolerance or encouragement of this characteristic.

Most professionals let their work and professionalism speak for themselves and don't feel any need to prove how smart they are. Pontificating, loud-mouthing, and arguing every point makes fundraising more arduous for everyone involved. It's also an easy way to ensure investors will grow annoyed, so work to ensure no one on your team is prone to that behavior.

Demonstrate Confidence, Not Arrogance

It is difficult to trust someone who acts like they are above it all. Arrogance can indicate a belief that one's own value will be the source of a company's success, rather than a team effort perfecting a product, applying a marketing strategy, and having a workable budget to support execution. Confidence, on the other hand, is a roundly desired attribute. Confidence is contagious. Confident people are more likely to persuade investors that their management team is prepared to handle the rigors and pressure of managing a start-up.

Arrogance can cause a range of outcomes that are difficult to predict and potentially costly. For example, when a person continues to pour money into a division that is going nowhere but they believe it's the right choice. That's not good. Whether the intentions are good or bad, they are rooted in arrogance. Pay attention to the character of the people you let into your company in its infancy.

While the line between arrogance and confidence is a fine one, it can be particularly so in business leaders (including founders, who are usually more confident than the average person). It's difficult to articulate the distinction, but you'll know it when you see it. Mark Cuban (*Shark Tank*) is confident; Elizabeth Holmes (Theranos) and Adam Neumann (WeWork) were arrogant.

Confident leaders speak their mind not for self-indulgence but for purpose, and they listen to others, too. Arrogant leaders are more prone to decision-making rationales centered on their own instincts. This sort of decision-making may not have investors rushing to hand over cash.

Willingly Learn from and Cooperate with Others

Every email, every call, every meeting, investors are getting an impression of you and your communication, leadership, and management skills. Over time, they will pick up on whether you genuinely seek input from others or are hesitant to follow anyone's guidance but your own.

Lone rangers' roles in corporate successes have been overemphasized in media. Mark Zuckerberg didn't build Facebook alone and Elon Musk isn't running the operations of multiple billion-dollar companies. Some people no doubt have extremely outsized effects and are the linchpin of the great successes of many companies, as both those individuals are. However, in none of those cases was every correct decision driven by that key person's imagination and skills of persuasion and execution. Teams and their productive functioning are what build successful companies. You want to show you understand this.

When leaders value what others offer, it is obvious, because others' insights are integrated into the business's strategy and operations. It is also obvious when leaders do not value others' input. Hopefully, you're a manager who surrounds yourself with competent people and listens to them (and doesn't let success change that). Jeff Bezos comes to mind. He started Amazon from nothing and is generally thought to have remained an inspirational and attentive leader as he and his team grew it into a household name.

No matter how smart you are and how well you know your business, your team will have useful ideas. Be sure to pay attention.

Time Is Money and Nobody Wants to Spend It on Self-Flattery

What people are really looking for is the rare breed of person who is sufficiently intelligent, works well with others, and comfortably accepts and adopts ideas superior to their own. The real world isn't TV. No one is looking for epic demonstrations of intellectual fortitude.

Showing off wastes time, and time really is money. When you're raising money, there is no time or money to waste. First, the whole process distracts management from attending to the most important parts of the business: its product or service, its market positioning, and the supporting operation. Any excess time spent on corporate finance matters is hampering the company's growth.

Second, the professionals involved in capital raises often bill by the hour. Four lawyers and one accountant on a call at $500 an hour each with twelve minutes wasted peacocking means a company has wasted about $500 that could have been spent more wisely.

Blown Raise Story: A Toxic Technology Officer

A recent engineering graduate was studying ways to improve the efficiency of electricity-generating windmills. Throughout his research, he discovered several novel ways to improve a windmill's performance, and he filed patents to protect these innovations. Shortly thereafter, while attending a green energy conference, he met a financial professional who was intrigued by his inventions. He told the recent graduate that his solutions were brilliant and that they should start a company and raise money to roll out applications of his technology around the world. The financial professional told him that with ideas this good, they would be making money in no time! Naturally, the graduate was excited and quickly agreed!

The financial professional reached out to his personal network and raised a round to fund the company's first year of operations that included a sales team to pitch the company's product solutions to wind power companies. The sales team called dozens of companies, but soon found they were encountering significant roadblocks. The sales cycle was long, and prospective buyers had questions about the quality of the technology coming from an emerging company.

When the sales team reported this back to the chief technology officer (our excited founding graduate), he was incensed. He told them that a competent sales team would be able to sell his brilliant solutions in under a week. He said their inability to close deals meant they were failures and would always be failures. He told them a product as phenomenal as the one he'd invented wasn't subject to sales cycles, and that they should all be fired for their incompetence.

When a junior associate tried to intervene, saying employees shouldn't be talked to like that, the chief technology officer lashed out and called her a moron. In fact, he took the position that this junior associate should also quit because she defended employees who were failures. Aghast, the junior associate told the financial founder that the chief technology officer's behavior was a problem, but he refused to act. He thought his co-founder was too important to the company and he would not know what to do if he left.

When the founders began approaching investors for their next funding round, they were surprised to find that many were asking about the company's rating on Glassdoor. Almost all the submissions related to the company on this popular site for jobseekers stated that the chief technology officer was a problem and would hobble the company's growth.

There were several instances where the chief technology officer was described as a toxic individual who chased away talent and who was a liability for the company. Investors started asking why so many employees were fired and hired over such a short period. The founders tried to spin the story as if the employees were the problem and sell the notion that they had made poor hiring decisions and needed to refocus on talent acquisition and retention. Unsurprisingly, with a wealth of data to the contrary, including clear evidence of employee turnover, investors weren't buying the story. Recognizing that the company had churned through so many employees due to a toxic work culture, investors realized their money might be better spent elsewhere.

18

Do Not Lie

PRESUMABLY YOU don't think the risk of ruining your company, leaving your professional and personal reputation in tatters, and potentially bankrupting yourself is worth the potential payoff of lying to investors. That's good, because you should never, under any circumstances, lie to or mislead a prospective investor.

You would think this goes without saying, but no. The unfortunate reality is, more entrepreneurs than you may expect lie to or mislead prospective investors. This can happen for a few reasons.

- Perhaps the entrepreneur has been knocking on doors and sending cold emails for months (or years) to no avail. She feels if she just stretches the truth about her accomplishments a little, she will get a meeting and convince the deep pockets to invest.
- Perhaps the company has a few warts (like an angry and resourceful ex-founder or an onerous legal dispute) and the entrepreneur feels if they wait to raise the issue until after the investor agrees to a deal and wires funds, the investor will see that these issues really aren't a big deal.

- Sometimes the founder is a bad egg who doesn't think lying is a big deal.

Reasons aside, every entrepreneur needs to know that the consequences of lying can be dire. Consequences will scale with the severity of the lie and the amount of money involved, especially when the investor discovers you lied to them to get (or, they might say, steal) their money. Elizabeth Holmes was "convicted of one count of conspiracy to commit fraud on investors and three counts of committing fraud on individual investors, which involved wire transfers totaling more than $140 million."[5] In general terms, she claimed Theranos was revolutionizing the possibilities for blood testing to identify diseases and raised money on that basis, but she did so knowing her company's technology was not working as she described.

If Your Lie Is Detected at the Outset

Entrepreneurs who lie can be caught rather early in the fundraising process, perhaps even during the first face-to-face interview or based on an initial review of the pitch deck. This shouldn't be surprising. Targeted investors will likely have a degree of expertise in your company's sector or technological application.

If an entrepreneur is caught lying at this stage, a patient investor may give an opportunity to clarify before closing the door, depending on the nature of the embellishment. Most, however, will write off the entrepreneur completely. There are consequences to this. Getting caught in a lie will not irritate only one investor.

Like every profession, investors have their own close-knit networks of colleagues, whether they are individual angels or work at established funds. These networks share investment opportunities with each other, ask for advice on deals, and warn each other when someone unscrupulous is looking for cash.

The consequences of lying to a single well-connected investor can reverberate throughout the investment community. You may find you've poisoned your reputation across a deeper well of prospects than you realized. Compounding this issue is that the network you poison might specialize in your specific industry or technology, potentially freezing you out of the group best equipped to understand your solution and drive returns. That's something you really want to avoid.

If Your Lie Is Detected during Due Diligence

If an investor likes your pitch, is satisfied with the results of their interviews, and wants to invest, they will likely commence their due diligence process to verify your business is as up to snuff as you've claimed. This process often involves bringing in third-party experts such as lawyers, accountants, consultants, PhDs, scientists, or other technical experts to pore over documents and assets.

The size of your raise, the maturity of your business, and the technical complexity of your operation are all factors that influence the cost of diligence. The cost can be modest, perhaps just a few thousand dollars for a new venture. For more mature and technical businesses, it can be significantly more (perhaps a few hundred thousand dollars).

Typically, the company is not required to pay any of these costs unless the investor invests (and then the costs are deducted from the proceeds). However, there is a common exception: if the investor discovers in the due diligence process that the entrepreneur lied to them.

When a material lie is uncovered during the due diligence process, the immediate consequence is that the investor will almost certainly walk away from the deal. Some investors may take this opportunity, if the business is otherwise truly promising, to harshly renegotiate the deal terms as punishment. However, the likelihood of that is extremely low. Most investors will view the relationship as irredeemable. Trust has been broken.

A tattered reputation may not be the only cost to the entrepreneur. Depending on how much the investor has spent on due diligence when the lie is discovered, and how vindictive they feel, they may pursue legal action against the company and the founder(s) personally to recuperate their costs. A poisoned reputation, no funding, and a bill that cannot be paid is no way to live.

If Your Lie Is Detected Post-Closing

Some companies have snuck lies past an investor, and through due diligence, and ended up with an investment. This phenomenon isn't restricted to small-money, early-stage entrepreneurs deceiving a lone investor with no diligence team. Plenty of significant start-ups (we've mentioned Theranos, but there are others, like Mozido) worth billions managed to secure investments by deceiving large teams of sophisticated professionals. What happens when you've received (and likely spent) an investor's check and they find out you lied to them to get their money? It depends.

If your business has performed poorly since funding and the investor realizes you duped them, they're likely to come after you. Lawsuits filed against the company and the founders are probably forthcoming; your investor will try to recuperate what they can. These lawsuits are an enormous managerial distraction, and the personal economic consequences can be devastating.

Alternatively, if your business has done well and its value has climbed considerably since the financing, and you're essential to that growth despite the web of lies, investors may be reticent to act. While they will be wary of trusting you ever again and will likely reserve the right to go after you if things don't work out, they may think it better to wait and see. If you're not *that* essential, they may maneuver to have you replaced.

Assuming you're essential, investors know that if they initiate a proceeding against you, it will negatively affect the company's business prospects, burn cash, and make it increasingly difficult for the company to raise more money. Many investors who find themselves in this position can be forced to bite their lip, as they know going after the company creates a lose-lose scenario. Don't count on this, though. At a certain point, everyone can be replaced.

Despite the famous adage, cheaters do sometimes prosper. Naturally, we do not want anyone to assume they will be this exception. Such thinking is playing with fire. If your company really is that special, you don't need to lie.

Remember, It's All about Trust

As we have repeated ad nauseum, investment requires trust.

If people don't trust you to steward their money in good faith, they won't write a check. There is no faster way to erode trust with anyone than by lying to them. Investors beyond the friends and family phase are unlikely to have any prior relationship with you that may facilitate forgiveness. In the real world, if a founder lies to investors and the investors find out, which one should assume they will, that founder is worthless from that moment on.

19

Consider Using an Advisory Board

WHEN AN early-stage company wants to raise money for a risky venture, that challenge can be exacerbated if its founders have little experience, gaps in their expertise, or limited credibility. The practical solution? Borrow someone else's experience, expertise, or credibility.

The common way to do this is by assembling a group of accomplished individuals, such as senior business types, tech entrepreneurs, or financial professionals who agree to serve on the company's advisory board. Many entrepreneurs use an advisory board in their quest to raise capital and build their business. Advisory boards can be helpful, but let's clear up what they actually do.

The Advisory Board vs. the Board of Directors

Advisory Board

When you're starting out and looking to raise those early rounds of capital, odds are your management team won't know how to do everything. No shame in that. Are there times your team could benefit from an outside perspective and the wisdom of experience? Definitely. Can you always afford to pay experienced people market rate for their time? Probably not.

Enter advisory boards, which are a collection of folks with specific expertise your team needs. As the name would suggest, advisory board members are there to provide advice and enhance your credibility. While board members will not show up to the office every day and run the business, most start-ups can benefit from having an advisory board.

The amount of time an advisory board member will dedicate varies tremendously. Some may be happy to chat for an hour a week and provide you with some truly engaged mentoring. Others will tell you not to call unless it is a crisis.

The term "board" in "advisory board" is somewhat misleading, because meetings almost never happen as a group. Rather, entrepreneurs often speak directly with individual members of the advisory board to access their unique expertise. There may be a group meeting once a year, or not at all.

For clarity, when people refer to an "advisory board," or say things like "she's on the advisory board" and so on, that is not the same thing as being on *the* board (of directors), which has the real power and duties.

Board of Directors

The board of directors we discussed earlier, often referred to simply as "the board," is a creature of statute (laws passed by legislatures). You'll recall that at the highest level, under corporate law, the board of directors is responsible for managing the affairs of a corporation. On that board, each member is a director and owes a fiduciary duty (i.e., must be seriously competent and loyal) to the corporation. Individual directors are often selected for their specific expertise, be it finance, compensation practices, or industry knowledge.

The directors meet as a group (the board), talk as a group, and vote and act on matters as a group. Matters such as whether to raise money or enter certain contracts. As a default, approval requires these decisions be voted for by majority at a meeting or otherwise consented to by the whole board in writing. The fiduciary duty of each director is serious stuff. They must act in the company's best interests and could face personal liability if they do not. Think of the board as a group of legal guardians for this creature of law, the corporation.

In contrast, advisory boards don't cast votes on big corporate decisions. They don't manage the affairs of the company. They just offer advice to the company's managers. They may not even a have formal contractual relationships with the company. They could just be a close family friend who wants to help by enhancing your credibility. What advisory board members don't have is a position imbued with significant statutory obligations! That's reserved for members of *the* board.

Do You Need an Advisory Board?

Whether you need an advisory board is something only you can answer, because the work of assembling and managing those relationships will fall to you. Do you feel you have a credibility gap you can shore up with some senior advisors? Do you feel investors will respond better to your pitch materials if they see a slide highlighting your advisors with connections into some of the biggest potential customers and suppliers in your industry? If it's a yes, putting one together could be a great move.

If you want an advisory board, reach out to your desired advisors early. Part of the benefit of having one is that when issues arise you'll have access to their knowledge and experience. Businesspeople are busy, and they will want time to consider whether they want to both dedicate a portion of their time to helping you and take on the limited, but nonetheless real, reputational risk accompanying association with your company. If an advisor will be featured in your pitch materials, they will want to ensure associating with you isn't likely to drag their name through the mud.

How Do You Assemble an Advisory Board?

Step one is to apply common sense. Think about what your management team is good at, what it isn't good at, and what expertise you could use. You may not know the answer to this question as thoroughly as you think. Ask people in your network for their input when trying to answer. Be sure to ask if they have any recommended advisors for your areas of need.

Step two is to consider what an investor might think you are missing. If you plan on shipping lots of product, but you're still in the development phase and have limited knowledge concerning logistics or supply chains, an advisor in this space could help you build a plan for this function and allay investors' concerns.

Once you know what expertise you need, step three is to identify folks by using your network and available tools (LinkedIn, alumni groups, etc.). Talk to people and ask for recommendations.

Step four is to begin outreach. Don't be afraid to make professional cold calls. Whether this process is smooth or rough is influenced by the strength of your network when you start, but anyone can do it with perseverance. It's likely your earliest advisors will come from your existing network, but you may be pleasantly surprised who is willing to help. You won't find out if you don't try. In our experience, advisory boards are assembled by entrepreneurs leveraging their existing relationships or networking in the fashion we've described above (i.e., getting introductions from people they already know or cold-calling folks who the founders think could be interested in getting involved).

Vet your candidates thoroughly. You may be tempted to stack the deck with big names to hook potential investors, but you must weigh the value of that benefit against the value you'll get from such folks. The time they will allocate to your venture compared to a less well-known advisor with comparable expertise may be significantly less. If they are keen and are committing significant time, great, but it's worth getting clarity up front. Investors aren't silly, and while a big name may get their attention, they're going to want to know how involved that person is planning to be. They need to understand the true value this person is offering and whether they fit with the organization.

Getting Legal with Advisors

When dealing with advisors who are close to you, especially relatives, it can be easy to forget you're dealing with a formal business relationship. You will need to paper up legal agreements covering a range of issues, including confidentiality and non-disclosure matters. You may even need some form of non-competition and non-solicitation of business relationships. Getting your advisors to agree to confidentiality and non-disclosure is fairly straightforward, but some will bristle at non-competes or non-solicits, depending on the specific legal language used and the advisory board member's other business activities. Whether you care will depend on the nature of your business, who the advisor is, and the associated risks you can tolerate.

Responsibilities

What are your advisors going to do? It's important to clarify this so everyone is on the same page. Many issues arise simply because people fail to align their expectations at the onset. Think about what you need from an advisor. Do you need their time or their connections? In terms of commitment, if you're expecting more than twenty hours of commitment a quarter, that's probably a bit much. However, if they're not willing to put up at least ten hours a quarter, you might question the value they're offering.

Compensation

Like any compensation package, the role of performance and time in driving aggregate compensation is up to the parties to discuss (and don't forget to do so). Recognize that advisors who are putting their name in your pitch deck are incurring reputational risk, and they reasonably expect to be compensated for that risk. Also, you want them to pick up your calls. Without some upside, they're unlikely to stay engaged.

Anecdotally, 0.25 to 1.25 percent of your company's equity for an advisor is an appropriate range (with the lower end being more common).[6] Don't forget that this equity should also be put on a vesting schedule in case the relationship doesn't work out. Everything is negotiable, though; this is just a benchmark.

Should Advisors Be Financially Invested?

It can be more than a little awkward to have big names on your advisory board, folks with lots of experience and career success (and presumably a little cash lying around), but when you're asked how much they have invested or plan to invest, your answer is "nothing." Receiving equity for time spent and paying for equity with cash signal very different things.

Merely sitting on an advisory board doesn't demonstrate the same level of confidence and commitment to a company as throwing down cash. Investors will be much more confident your advisors will pick up the phone when you call if they've put up their own money. Whichever way you go, have an explanation ready.

Get to It

In summary, consider whether you could use an advisory board. If so, use your network to form and document it and decide on the role advisors will play. Once formed, use it, don't ignore it, and stay in communication with your advisors. Regular and reasonable communication may be the single greatest behavior a person can rely on to maintain good working relationships.

20

Chart Clear Milestones and Goals

DO YOU dream of resting on a balcony, absorbing a beautiful sunset, freed by the knowledge you never *have* to work again? That's cool, but even if you achieve that goal (we hope you do!), it is probably years away. And no matter how stoic you are, a goal whose accomplishment is years away can be difficult to hold on to without something to celebrate in between. It can be harder still for your team, who need to celebrate accomplishments along the way. To keep your team motivated, give them clear guidance on how their work will realize the company's vision.

Think of milestones as intermediate steps on the path to completing goals. When Netflix decided to upend the antiquated video rental industry, its *goal* might have been to reign supreme over movie- and television-watching eyeballs by offering folks a digital service with a library of movies and shows accessible from the couch. But its first *milestone* might have been drafting a basic outline of a digital platform capable of delivering the core components of its proposed service. However you break it down, the point is to create a detailed plan outlining the important steps to achieving your goal.

Investors Objectively Evaluate Your Company

In each fundraising round investors will want to see how financially prudent you were in completing your previously established milestones. Be disciplined and prepared to talk about your company's performance with reference to them.

This may feel unnecessary to you because of how close you are to the business, but it is helpful for those not as intertwined in the daily functioning. That's not their role. Theirs is to provide capital and certain other support, such as connections to potential employees and assistance negotiating partnerships. Part of your job is to help them understand what the business they invested in is doing and how their money is being used. This way they can understand, help address problems, and evaluate whether to invest more.

Milestones are equalizers. No matter how much better you understand your business than your investors, if you agree that certain milestones are reasonable and yet continually fail to achieve them, the implication is clear. Milestones give investors valuable pieces of information to evaluate your performance against and decide how to handle their investment in your company going forward.

To be fair, each milestone's complexity will factor into this decision. If you failed to achieve something because you decided to start a band, there will be a drought of sympathy. If, on the other hand, you're uncovering complexities that any innovator in the space would face, and therefore require more financial and human capital than originally expected, the sympathy (and cash) may not dry up so quickly.

Know Where You're Going

Putting aside investors' interests for a moment, it's difficult to get where you're going if you can't tell whether you're making progress. Setting clear goals, and the intermediate milestones necessary to achieve those goals, helps you set your direction, see what you need to do to get there, and learn how to measure your progress along the way.

Practically speaking, it's best to set realistic timelines. A person whose plans take into account the realities of life (at work and home) is instantly a favorite among their colleagues. While it's not your goal to be liked, it is your goal to keep people working for you. People prefer working for someone they like.

One of the greatest frustrations among professionals in modern business culture is the seemingly endless absence of realism when setting timelines. True, sometimes a full-court press is needed. There can be real reasons why timing needs to be "yesterday," but we all read "The Boy Who Cried Wolf" as kids. When everything is a fire drill, nothing is. It seems that in the process of earning fancy degrees, some professionals forgot the simple wisdom childhood bestowed.

Writing down and tracking your progress on your milestones will help you and your team visualize what you need to do in the short term, and it will give you a clear sense of where you're going in the long term. It will also minimize the frustrations that being rushed to finish tasks on a tight deadline cause your team, which will help you with employee retention (a huge cost saver).

Set Clear Milestones

Clear milestones such as a functional prototype, the first customer contract, a certain number of users, or a revenue target help with focus and give direction, and they are also satisfying to complete. Passing checkpoints keeps you going in pursuit of the grander vision. If your only goal is to reach your IPO, the frustration of the wait is likely to weigh on you. It will not be a particularly helpful motivator during the darkest days.

Don't underestimate the importance of morale and a collective sense of progress. Break projects into their components, celebrate progress, and present those components visually to your team. Keep people motivated and their milestones clearly defined in the context of the larger set of goals.

If you're leading, it's your job to keep your organization engaged and focused on achieving its milestones. It's important to be positive and excited about incremental achievements while continuing unabated pursuit of the endgame. Business is different from politics in that you can stop to celebrate achievements without some buzzkill chastising you for celebrating while there is still work to be done. You don't have to be miserable until you're standing on the ashes of every blockade between you and your dreams.

Enhance Accountability

Milestones are also a handy means of enforcing accountability in your organization. They can reveal where more attention may be needed (and, therefore, what teams may need more help—or, in the worst case, restructuring). Tracking milestones and their achievement creates measurable datapoints to study your operation, improve process efficiencies, and develop internal resources related to project management and execution.

Also, as we alluded to above, investors will use the objective truth of whether you are achieving your milestones to hold you accountable. If you fail to hit milestones, they may turn off the money supply or take other legal options. How can they trust you to deliver returns if you can't accomplish the necessary steps to your larger goal? To them it will seem like they are throwing good money after bad.

You may have noticed that this whole chapter can be summed up as: keep a to-do list for making your vision a reality, and celebrate achieving the items on that list. We highly recommend you do exactly that.

21

"Guarantee" Nothing

YOUR TEAM has worked hard fine-tuning your pitch. You have a tight and persuasive delivery to win over even the most hardened investor. One of your co-founders, who spends far too much time online, recalls an old commercial where a salesman closes his pitch by looking at the camera and saying, "I guarantee it." You think this would be a fantastic line to bake into your pitch.

Please do not say this. We can "guarantee" the potential financial consequences are not worth whatever presentation value you see in the line.

Disclaim and Qualify

As a confident entrepreneur, it's understandable why you might want to use language like "guaranteed," "assured," or "no question" when describing your future financial performance. All investors have their doubts about new opportunities, and you want to signal confidence. The problem is, this language, in the worst cases, may create considerable liability for losses your investors might incur.

Experienced fundraisers understand this liability, which is why properly prepared investor presentations include extensive up-front disclaimers. Before the reader sees anything about the actual business, the disclaimer has cautioned them that any "forward-looking" information in the materials are projections, and emphasized that no assurance can be given that anything they are about to read will happen. This disclaimer can be a few paragraphs or several pages, but the heart of the message is the same: the contents contain a considerable degree of uncertainty and the company's future performance is not guaranteed.

Notwithstanding the disclaimer, you may notice executives routinely pepper their presentations with qualifiers to emphasize that the contents are management projections only, not assured results. Qualifying words such as "anticipated," "estimated," and "potential" are layered throughout materials. Instead of saying management's new marketing efforts "will lead to increased sales," it's better to say something like "are expected to lead to increased sales."

On occasion, companies cite third-party research to support the case that their industry presents a hyper-growth opportunity. Accordingly, you will likely see pronounced citations clarifying that this information is from a third party and management may be relying on the accuracy of that information in their own projections.

While this level of caveating may seem over the top, it is designed to protect the entrepreneur and provide a clear warning to the investor. Given the risk associated with accidentally using the wrong language, what should you do as an entrepreneur to ensure you do not make this mistake?

A Lawyerly Review

It is best practice to send your pitch materials to a corporate lawyer before circulating them to prospective investors. A review by trained eyes can ensure you have not accidentally implied that any potential financial performance presented is in any way assured. Even if you think you can do this on your own by screening for certain words, you might be surprised to realize that certain seemingly harmless phrases can create liability.

Some entrepreneurs who have gone through financing rounds may tell you, "this worrying is unnecessary," or "a waste of money," but they're not on the line if things go sideways. If you are concerned about cost, an experienced lawyer can carve through your pitch materials and make the necessary edits and recommendations in a fairly short period of time (one to three hours, depending on its length). The disclaimers you would slap on the first page of your pitch deck and any accompanying financial model are fairly boilerplate. Your lawyer generally won't need to draft a new one; they'll just check for any obvious gaps or replace it wholesale with their standard language.

Some entrepreneurs charge forward without legal review and purposefully include statements like "we will be the market leader in two years" with the hope of winning dollars. When entrepreneurs make this decision, they could be exposing the company to unnecessary risk, hinging on the company's success and the investor's temperament. It's not the most prudent path.

Consequences

Most reasonable investors have seen wins and losses and understand most of their high-risk bets will not pan out. Unfortunately, not all investors are reasonable when money is lost. This is true particularly if an investor is new to investing in start-ups and doesn't realize things can become truly worthless, with their entire investment wiped out and no hope of recovery. At the end of the day investors are people, and some people can become difficult in stressful circumstances where money is involved.

Investors who feel (or can argue) they were misled or duped because of language in presentation materials might be vindictive enough to sue you in a personal capacity. Entrepreneurs who shrug off the threat of personal lawsuits by enraged investors tend to fall into one of a few camps: they don't think their business will fail, don't believe the investor would ever sue, or think no one would sue them because they don't have any money.

In reality, any business can fail under the right circumstances, which may be out of anyone's control. In that situation, when large financial losses are involved, people you think you know well can turn in a moment. Just because you have no personal assets to lose does not mean people won't sue you. Plenty of people will try to get blood from a stone if they are sufficiently motivated or incensed. This motive doesn't necessarily have to be that an investor lost all their money. Your company may very well become profitable, but someone may still come after you personally if your actual results fall materially short of the ones you guaranteed. How awful would that be?

Entrepreneurs do not need to add unnecessary risk to their lives just to make their pitch more convincing. Quite frankly, if you have decided to launch your own business, you have taken on more than enough risk, so don't guarantee anything.

22

Don't Pay Yourself Too Much

YOU AND your co-founders will be critical to the company's initial success. Whether you are the right management team to carry out your plan will be a huge investor consideration. Collectively, you will be tasked with product development, managing considerable sums of investor money, prudently allocating resources, hiring top talent, and implementing the company's growth strategy.

Bearing this in mind, you do some research and see the average executive in your industry earns a cash salary of several hundred thousand dollars per year. Given the enormity of the challenge ahead, you may feel it's reasonable to compensate yourself in a similar fashion. If you take this approach, do not be surprised when investors aren't interested.

It Is All about Alignment

On occasion, an investor who likes your company, your idea, and your team will pay no mind to how much you and your team are paying yourselves. Don't assume you will raise exclusively from this minority. We'd hazard to say there is not a single (competent) fund that will not review management's compensation before they write a check. In that review, they will look for alignment between their interests and the risk-reward opportunity the founding managers are embracing.

You have undertaken a huge risk by launching a new business, and your investors are taking an enormous risk by betting on you. You both stand to make a lot of money if things go well, but first they need to go well. Meaning, you can't be overpaid as if you're the CEO of Microsoft right away. A cushy salary won't properly incentivize you to keep your nose to the grindstone and build the business.

Investors know things often go very poorly for venture investments. While they hope their investment will multiply, they understand it may also go to zero. Investors do not want situations where a company fails and disintegrates their investment but the founders still walk away with ample cash savings from generous salaries. This does not mean investors do not want to see you get rich. They simply want you to become rich in a manner that makes them rich, too.

Your investors want you to get rich from increasing the value of the shares you hold in the company. As your company rises in value, your investors accrue bragging rights for being able to spot winning companies (useful for attracting other companies to invest in and other limited partners to give them money) and they become richer. So, how do investors ensure alignment when making their investment?

Say on Pay

In any financing round, the investors will likely have powerful influence on executive compensation matters. As a condition for making their investment, savvy investors often demand specific salary levels, especially if the company is younger and less established.

This is critical to remember because you may plan on luring some of your prospective co-founders on the basis of a certain salary. You can imagine how ugly the conversation could become if you promised to match a friend's salary if they left their current job, only for them to discover they will make barely half of that. Sadly, if this happens, you could be in the market for a new friend.

Admittedly, some investors are excessively hawkish when setting founder salaries—$60,000 per year isn't going to cut it in the Bay Area if you have a family, but you shouldn't expect $300,000 in the early stages either. After all, they know every dollar going to you in salary is one less dollar going into other key corporate activities such as research, marketing, and product development. That said, most investors recognize you still need to pay for talent. There is a fine line between aligning incentives and scaring founders.

If an investor demands punishingly low salaries as a condition of their investment, they run the risk you will instead approach another investor. Even worse, they may put their money into a company only for all the founders to take second jobs to pay their bills. In this scenario, the investor's cash is stuck in a business whose key leadership team is contributing only a fraction of the time required for it to be successful.

Setting Expectations (for Yourself and Others)

If you hit the road with unreasonable salary demands, some investors will dismiss you on that basis alone. It presents as grossly out of touch with market realities and the company's circumstances, which are not traits an investor wants in a key executive. So, to avoid this problem, how much salary should you ask for?

There is no universal dollar amount for how much founders should pay themselves, as every person's circumstances differ. If you have children or work in a city with high living costs, your needs will differ from founders living in greener pastures without little ones. Approach the problem by establishing how much you need to take home to ensure your full attention is focused on the business. A salary requiring you to moonlight at a local fast-food restaurant to make rent is too little. But if you are thinking beyond rainy-day savings to your next Tahitian vacation, it is probably too much. What this number looks like will be very different from Atlanta to Toronto to Calgary to San Francisco.

If you're struggling to nail down a number for your salary (or anyone else's, for that matter), Carta Total Comp is a product that can help an entrepreneur ensure they are setting appropriate compensation packages. Using current data from tens of thousands of companies, a founder can benchmark against any role, level, and region to establish what you should pay, including salary and equity incentives, and what peer companies are paying. It also has tools for communicating with employees regarding their compensation packages. These insights and functions could be valuable for hiring and retention.

Remember that the salary you set when you first raise capital is not set in stone. As the business grows and you demonstrate managerial prudence, there will be opportunities to renegotiate a rate more commensurate with the company's success and your skill level. However, these later opportunities will never arise if you demand compensation at the onset as if you've already grown the business to success.

Blown Raise Story: A Tale of Two Dentists

A medical device start-up founded by two dentists was looking for a CEO to run the business and handle the company's first financing. The dentists developed a patent for a new device, but quickly realized they needed a professional business operator for their company to succeed.

They recruited an extremely talented and experienced medical device executive who had recently left a corner office at one of North America's largest medical device companies following its acquisition. Understandably, this executive had certain compensation expectations. After the dentists refused to give him any shares, he negotiated for an annual cash salary of $500,000. Because the founding dentists, who had never been through a fundraising round and would not be doing any work for the company, kept all the company's shares to themselves, the only upside for the new executive was his salary.

Soon the executive presented a plan to raise just over $1.5 million to fund the first twelve months of operations and began approaching investors. When prospective investors realized one-third of their money was going to just one individual, who had no equity stake in the company he was supposed to lead, things quickly turned sour. With the CEO poised to take so much cash off the table from a company with no revenue, no product to sell, and no managerial incentive for growth, it shouldn't surprise you that no investors emerged.

23

Crowdfunding May Not Be "Easier"

MANY PEOPLE have ready access to tools to buy shares in a publicly traded company. It isn't difficult to open a brokerage account, deposit funds, and purchase a given stock, regardless of someone's wealth or income. The rules for investing in private companies (i.e., companies whose shares do not trade on a stock exchange), however, are more limiting.

Many countries have extensive restrictions on who can invest in privately owned companies. Nominally, the underlying goal is to protect ordinary folks from being fleeced or defrauded by unscrupulous business types preying on people's naïveté about the risks of investing in private companies (particularly start-ups). That is not to say that unscrupulous business types who work at public companies do not prey on ignorant people. The thought is that because public companies have extensive disclosure requirements while most private companies do not, ordinary folks are protected when they invest in these public companies. Regardless of whether this logic, which places disclosure on a pedestal, holds up in practice, the powers that be decided, with only a handful of exceptions, that investing in private companies is generally limited to friends, family, and investors who are considered "accredited."

Who qualifies as an accredited investor varies from country to country and continues to evolve. At the heart of the definition is the concept that you must possess a certain level of wealth or earn a certain level of income—and those amounts are hefty. The idea is that wealthier people have a greater ability to absorb major losses. Supposedly, they are also more financially sophisticated. Some may say it is as if, by law, only the rich can get richer.

Given some of the inherent weaknesses in this logic, in the United States, the definition of "accredited investor" was recently expanded to include individuals with certain professional certifications. This was partially due to many people criticizing the fact that a wealthy person who may have inherited all their money and knows zero about business could invest in private companies, while less well-off people with professional financial certifications who are trying to build wealth could not.

Over the past several years, the movement to allow more people to invest early in private companies, regardless of their wealth or income, has contributed to the rise of crowdfunding. Crowdfunding is a concept that allows companies to raise money by securing small investments from many investors, typically through an organized online portal. Governments are still keenly focused on preventing fraud involving large sums of money, which is why many have capped the maximum amount a single person can invest in crowdfunding situations. Despite this, the legal emergence of crowdfunding has presented a new opportunity for entrepreneurs seeking capital.

Types of Crowdfunding

Broadly speaking, there are two types of crowdfunding campaigns that emerging companies may partake in: those providing contributors with products or services, and those providing contributors with a share of a company's financial success.

Entrepreneurs, whether they are running a company or are an individual artist or content creator, can look to crowdfunding when they have a product they want to sell to retail consumers but lack the funds to make the product available. For example, a comic book creator may have drafted a comic, but has no funds on hand to publish the work. The creator could use crowdfunding to raise money and send contributors a physical comic book in exchange for their contribution. Conveniently, this approach allows the creator to print the exact number required and avoid piling up unnecessary inventory.

This is effectively a form of inventory financing, which is a practice where companies get short-term financing to purchase inventory for prospective customers. The difference is, the financing comes from the customers rather than a lender. Instead of paying interest to a third-party lender, the artist pays a commission to the crowdfunding platform.

The second type of crowdfunding is when an entrepreneur sells a stake in the financial success of their company. In these campaigns, entrepreneurs typically offer contributors company stock and follow many of the same steps they would with other investors. This includes setting a raise amount, articulating the company's valuation, and providing key investment documents for review. Some companies raise debt through crowdfunding platforms, but equity raises are more common, as lending even small amounts of money to emerging companies comes with many unique challenges.

There are many reasons why entrepreneurs may choose to raise equity financing through a crowdfunding platform instead of engaging with funds or high-net-worth individuals. Some entrepreneurs recognize they are developing a product or service with a passionate fanbase and many of these fans would be interested in owning a piece of the company. That contingent of fans/investors can be a powerful source of leverage for founders who graduate to later financing rounds.

Many crowdfunders appreciate the simplicity of organizing everything digitally and developing a single campaign that does not require them to court well-monied investors with custom materials. Others may crowdfund because they believe they can get a fan premium, translating into a better valuation compared to the terms they might get from a well-heeled fund. Finally, and unfortunately, one misguided reason many entrepreneurs crowdfund is that they think it will be easy. The process is anything but.

It's worth noting there are certain limitations to crowdfunding. For example, in the U.S., the maximum amount that can be raised under Regulation CF in a crowdfunding campaign by a company during any twelve-month period is $5 million. Individuals who are not accredited investors can invest up to a cap between $2,200 and $107,000 in all Regulation CF campaigns; their exact cap is based on their income and net worth. In Canada that limit is C$1.5 million. While securities laws vary by province, National Instrument 45-110 (Start-up Crowdfunding Registration and Prospectus Exemptions) provides that individual investors (who are not accredited investors) can invest only up to $2,500 per crowdfunding offering.

Take It Seriously

The biggest mistake you can make in a crowdfunding campaign is thinking it will necessarily be "easier" than raising money from more conventional sources, such as angel investors or venture funds. Entrepreneurs may think they will face less scrutiny from crowdfunding investors than from a fund. While it is true that with crowdfunding you may evade needling questions on your share structure, you will face a new problem: standing out among the sea of other crowdfunding opportunities. There are always trade-offs.

Crowdfunding requires a marketing and engagement plan detailing how you will attract ordinary people to invest in your opportunity. Few things are worse for a company than announcing that a crowdfunding campaign has gone live and nobody shows up to buy. In crowdfunding, momentum attracts investors, so if you're receiving a slow trickle of funds, you may find yourself unable to hit your minimum amount required to close, leaving you with no money whatsoever. That's right: crowdfunding campaigns have target amounts, and if the raise doesn't reach its minimum amount, the company won't get any money.

Generally, you want to build a groundswell of excitement before your raise goes live, so that when it does, a flood of investors sign up from day one. It is not as simple as posting targeted advertisements to buy your company's shares on a certain day. Your marketing plan must not run afoul of any securities laws, which may severely punish the non-compliant promotion of securities. If you are raising on a less-trafficked platform, in addition to convincing folks to invest, you may also need to convince them to open an account with the investing platform in advance.

All the while, you still need to stand out among companies competing for the same investors' dollars. Even if the other companies do not make the same product as you, they may be operating in your industry or appealing to investors with similar interests. The point is, the amount of planning and legwork required for a successful crowdfunding campaign is not necessarily easier than tapping more conventional sources.

Other things to consider include the fact that most crowdfunding platforms we mentioned (Netcapital, Wefunder, and the other online marketplaces we mentioned in the Who's Who) make money by charging a commission or portal fee. This commission can often sit in the 7 to 8 percent range of your total raise. Some platforms charge more and some less. There can also be ancillary service and transaction fees to consider, so do your costing due diligence. This can be a big deal, because if you do not account for these costs, you may inadvertently raise an amount insufficient to meet your company's funding requirements net of the commission.

One additional item: if you are developing a new technology, you must speak with an intellectual property lawyer before uploading any details about it to a crowdfunding platform or data room. Posting intimate details about your technology without consulting a professional and potentially filing for the necessary legal protections can jeopardize your company's commercial potential.

If you manage to execute a successful crowdfunding campaign, you'll realize that anyone who thinks it is necessarily "easier" is misguided. This doesn't mean it can't be the right choice for a company or that it can't be easier than a conventional raise. The easiest crowdfunding campaign would certainly be better than the worst traditional raise. All we're saying is, don't fall into the trap of believing it's necessarily an easier alternative than the traditional venture capital route.

Managing Retail Investors

One of the clearest differences between raising money from a crowdfunding campaign compared to a VC fund are the type and number of your shareholders. Given the restrictions in crowdfunding on how much money can be raised from each individual investor, you may find yourself with hundreds, potentially even thousands, of shareholders if you raise a decent chunk of change.

All these investors will be "retail" investors, which means they are individuals investing their own money, who will have varying degrees of business and financial acumen. Some may work at funds and be professional investors by day, and others will have no financial education whatsoever. Contrast this with institutional investors, like venture capital funds, who invest other people's money and have institutional financial expertise.

A major challenge with having so many retail investors is that their disparity in business knowledge can require you to spend more time than you expected on shareholder relations. You may have well-meaning but ignorant shareholders bombard you with questions. Simply ignoring them to focus on the business is not going to help you either, because irritating these shareholders can lead to public vocalizations of displeasure with their investment. You would be right to point out that this is self-defeating, given that they are investors and have an interest in you succeeding, but it can happen, so you must plan to ensure it does not happen to you.

To hammer it home: a crowdfunding campaign can be a great way to raise capital, but don't make the mistake of taking the work that goes into it, both before and after you raise, lightly.

24

Big Risks Require Big Rewards

A BASIC PREMISE of investing is that the relative risk of any opportunity needs to be commensurate with the potential reward. You've no doubt heard some formulation of the phrase, "the greater the risk, the greater the reward." In the investing world, this means reasonable investors willing to participate in high-risk opportunities expect a pathway—not a guarantee, but a pathway—to realizing returns among the highest level of any asset class.

Gambling odds illustrate the relationship between risk and return. If you bet straight up on a single number on an American roulette wheel, you will have just a 1 in 38 chance of winning. That's a low probability, but if you hit your number and win big, you will make 35 times your bet! Said another way, you could make a 3,500 percent return on a spin of a wheel. High risk, high reward.

Obviously, these odds do not favor the gambler (the house needs to win most of the time), but the potential reward for the gambler is at least commensurate with the accepted risk. Similarly, national and state lotteries offer participants the chance to multiply the purchase price of a lottery ticket by a factor of several million. Of course, the buyer faces infinitesimally small odds of winning. Now, imagine if one of those lotteries offered you only the chance to double your money with a one in one million chance to win; you would probably play something else. One in a million odds of turning $2 into $4 isn't that enticing—you'd basically be giving away the $2.

Reasonable investors recognize that any investment in a new enterprise, even if the product or service coming to market is extremely compelling, has a substantial risk of being a loss. The journey from starting and growing a small company into a profitable enterprise includes countless business risks, which is why so many fail. Even if an entrepreneur is launching a great product into what they believe is a low-risk sector with well-understood economics, the execution risk involved in building a business remains significant. This explains in part why VC funds are generally looking to invest in companies offering at least a 10X return to its earliest VC investors.[7]

Liquidity

Elevating the degree of risk for the investor beyond the business risk is the issue of liquidity. When invested in large publicly traded companies, like Tesla, investors who dislike the direction of the company can sell their investment any time when the applicable market(s) are open. If an investment can be readily sold and converted into cash without suffering a material drop on the value of the investment, it is "liquid." There is a premium demanded by investors related to their ability to sell (called a liquidity premium), which is baked into the stock price. The greater the inability for the investor to sell, the higher the return they will demand (i.e., the higher the liquidity premium). For most start-ups, their securities are very difficult to sell, meaning they are illiquid.

Despite the attention of venture investing, active markets for shares in early-stage start-ups are still small, and the transfer restrictions often imposed before the company has been sold or gone public (more on this later) can make selling the shares a non-starter. This means investors who participate in an early-stage round must accept that they are in it for the relatively long haul. These equity securities are priced with an illiquidity discount, and early investors get the benefit of that discount as compensation for the liquidity risk.

Rates of Return

While most entrepreneurs inherently understand that the general business risk and liquidity risk associated with start-ups require higher rates of return, a question many entrepreneurs have when pitching investors is this: What exactly is a reasonable rate of return that an investor might expect for a high-risk emerging opportunity? You clearly don't want to make a grossly out-of-touch pronouncement that will have you shown the door, but you also don't want to give away the farm. Before we address the specific level of returns expected, it's best to discuss how investors think about returns.

Investors assess their investment opportunities from different angles, including the quality of the management team, the strength of the product or service, and the overall product-market fit. But what they really want to know is how much money they could make if everything goes well.

Return on Investment

You may assume investors just want to know how much they are putting in and how much they will get back. This thinking describes what is technically known as the Return on Investment (ROI). ROI, which is (deceptively) simple to calculate, summarizes in one number the total return an investor could earn on their invested capital over the life of the investment. Expressed as a percentage, one way to calculate ROI is:

Return on Investment = ([Exit Value of Investment – Initial Investment] / Initial Investment) × 100

You subtract the Initial Investment from the Exit Value of Investment because before you can have a return *on* your investment, you first need a return *of* your investment.

An example of this equation in action would be if someone invested $1 million for an equity stake in a company at a $4 million pre-money valuation. With the additional $1 million, the post-money valuation is $5 million; the investor's stake is one-fifth, or 20 percent. If that company goes on to sell for $25 million (without the need for additional fundraising or employee stock issuances), that investor's 20 percent equity stake would generate an ROI of 400 percent: $5 million (20 percent, or one-fifth, of $25 million) minus the initial $1 million investment yields a profit of $4 million, 4x the initial investment. Alternatively, if things went poorly and the company sold for just $2 million, the exit value of that investors' 20 percent equity would be just $400,000. In this case, the ROI is negative 60 percent; the $1 million investment lost 60 percent ($600,000) of its value.

Time Value of Money and Internal Rate of Return

While ROI can seem relatively easy and straightforward to calculate, sophisticated investors will never use ROI in a venture context. Why not? Because the equation above does not account for what is known as the time value of money. "Time value of money" refers to the concept that money received sooner is worth more than money received later. For example, if someone offered you an investment with an expected ROI of 50 percent and you invested, you'd probably be thrilled if you received your return the next year. What if you didn't receive your return for fifteen years? Obviously you'd be much less happy. That difference in satisfaction is the time value of money.

The Internal Rate of Return, or IRR, accounts for the time value of money, which is why investors of all stripes—from venture funds to pensions—consider the IRR when evaluating investments. Essentially, investors want to know what their forecasted return is based on the cash flows they invest and receive over their anticipated holding period, and they want to see that return metric expressed on an annualized basis. This forecasted return is the IRR.

The premise is quite simple. IRR is driven by just four things: (1) the amount of cash you invest, (2) when your cash is invested, (3) how much cash you receive back from the investment, and (4) when cash is distributed back to you. The more cash you get back from your investment and the sooner it comes, the higher the IRR. On the flip side, the less cash you get back and the longer it takes to get it, the lower the IRR. Determining IRR with a calculator or software like Microsoft Excel is relatively straightforward. The table below illustrates the calculation of IRR for two different scenarios, where the initial investment of $2 million is followed by a total of $5.9 million in cash returned to an investor.

Cash Flow Date	Cash Flow Profile 1	Cash Flow Profile 2
31-Dec-21	($2,000,000)	($2,000,000)
31-Dec-22	$400,000	$1,400,000
31-Dec-23	$700,000	$1,750,000
31-Dec-24	$400,000	$1,250,000
31-Dec-25	$1,250,000	$400,000
31-Dec-26	$1,750,000	$700,000
31-Dec-27	$1,400,000	$400,000
IRR	**31.83%**	**60.62%**

Parentheses indicate a negative number.

Notice that when the larger cash flows come sooner, the IRR is higher despite the fact that the total cash flow is the same? Again, that's the time value of money. It is worth noting, however, that in the venture context there aren't likely to be multiple cash flows to investors. Rather, there will be one large cash flow at the exit.

VC Compensation and Expected Returns

Perhaps the most glaringly obvious challenge with both ROI and IRR is how exceptionally difficult it is to predict the exit value of an investment, especially when investing in high-risk companies like start-ups. Calculating the exit value on a one-year bond issued by a government with a great credit rating? Not a problem. Calculating the exit value on a highly speculative tech company with no working product, a shifting regulatory environment, and substantial uncertainty regarding market adoption? Yikes. Where to begin?

A good starting point is to understand how the VC's management team—which we will refer to as the general partner, since most VCs are structured as limited partnerships—makes money. Understanding these mechanics will help you get a sense of the level of returns they expect. The first component of the general partner's compensation for its work managing the VC fund is in the form of management fees. Management fees can be calculated as a simple percentage of the total investment dollars committed to the fund. These fees pay for the salaries and overhead costs (rent, utilities, etc.) to operate the fund.

The second component of their compensation is the one that really matters. It allows the general partner to participate in the VC fund's returns and earn big money. This component is referred to as the "carried interest," which you may have heard politicians yelling about. How does carried interest work? Under the limited partnership agreement between the general partner and the limited partners of the VC fund, the general partner gets a specified share of the returns generated by the VC fund's investments, typically after the limited partners have received some minimum threshold return.

The carried interest is essentially the GP's share of the fund profits. Depending on the fund, the GP normally earns anywhere from 10 to 20% of the fund's profits. Maximizing fund profit and therefore the carried interest is where the big money is, and is the goal toward which all funds are managed. In fact, senior members of the GP's management team will typically be entitled to a portion of the carried interest, which further ensures that their decision making mirrors the overall objective of the fund while minimizing investment losses and maximizing the returns from the fund's successful companies.

So, now that you understand how the general partner is paid, exactly what level of expected returns are they looking for from a prospective investment to write a check? The top quartile of VC funds generate annual returns (i.e., an IRR) around 25 percent, so given that many VC funds' prospective investments might fail, investment targets need to offer returns far beyond that level. VCs are looking to invest in opportunities that can blow past their average returns, especially when investing in a company's earliest rounds, so when you are at your earliest stages of development, offering an opportunity to earn only a top fund's average return isn't offering much of anything.

Given all of this, an enticing approach is to illustrate a scenario where your company significantly outperforms the average returns of a successful VC fund. In other words, you need to offer them an IRR well beyond 25 percent. You may encounter investors who say they "only" invest in companies that may become unicorns (a company whose valuation crosses the $1 billion mark and potentially generates a three-digit IRR), but pay them no mind. Most rational venture investors recognize that if you offer them an opportunity to exceed the returns of an average fund in the top quartile of VC funds, you are presenting a worthwhile opportunity.

Triangulation

As we mentioned, calculating the exit value of a speculative start-up investment is no easy task. Experienced investors don't expect to nail down a precise value. They get comfortable with an estimated range. If they wanted a high degree of certainty, they would invest in low-risk assets like government and corporate debt, where the return is entirely predictable except in the most extreme circumstances (like war). But that's not the market VC funds are in. They're shooting for the stars. They're taking big risks to get big rewards.

In the absence of a crystal ball, venture investors rely on several different methods to triangulate the potential range of values they may realize on an investment at exit. These methods include:

- **Public comparables.** While no two companies are the same and each has its own unique story, they all have competitors or peers engaged in a similar pursuit, relying on similar business models, with similar cost structures. These are "comparables." Depending on the industry, many of these companies may already be publicly traded—for example, on the Nasdaq. Publicly listed companies must disclose a plethora of information, including financial statements and the value of their shares (i.e., the stock price). Investors can use this available information about your company's comparables to infer your company's potential value if it achieves certain operational or financial milestones. They can also use proprietary information about other companies they have come into contact with.
- **Precedent transactions.** Going public is not the most common way companies provide a pathway for their earliest investors to cash out. Most start-ups that exit are sold to larger companies before they ever list their shares on a stock exchange, and the values of comparable companies sold in the public markets offer guidance on valuation (and in turn, investors' expected returns). If your company's comparables in a certain sector are selling within a certain range of multiples of their annual revenues or profit (or other metrics), those multiples provide a basis for investors to estimate what your company could sell for to a potential acquirer. A VC fund will have its own proprietary set of precedent transactions that it will likely consider as well.

- **Your projections.** Your operational and financial projections are deeply influenced by your assumptions, interpretations and, most significantly, biases. That said, just because your potential investor understands this influence doesn't mean they will write off your projections entirely. Investors will take your projections into account when considering how your unique circumstances differ from those publicly traded companies and precedent company sales, and how those differing circumstances influence the valuation multiples of revenue, profits, or other metrics they should apply when valuing your business. They will consider how whatever unique solution you have developed differs from what has been disclosed publicly and whether those points of differentiation offer the potential for enhanced value capture.

When considering what returns investors are expecting, you want to think about what businesses investors will be comparing to yours to gauge the potential of the investment opportunity you are presenting. They will consider a wealth of data, and you owe it to yourself to connect the dots. If a comparable company is generating an annual net operating cash flow of $50 million and its total equity value is $850 million (a 17X multiple of net operating cash flow), you can use that information to get some sense of what you're offering.

Perhaps you expect to be generating $20 million in annual operating cash flow in three years, and you're asking for a $10 million investment for 15 percent of your company. On that basis, you may tell the investor you estimate your company's equity could be worth $340 million ($20 million multiplied by 17) in three years. With their 15 percent stake growing to $51 million, you're offering the opportunity for the investor to earn a 72 percent IRR, assuming an exit occurs on December 31, 2024.

Cash Flow Date	Cash Flow Profile
31-Dec-21	($10,000,000)
31-Dec-22	$ -
31-Dec-23	$ -
31-Dec-24	$51,000,000
IRR	72.13%

Of course, this is an extremely oversimplified example, and there are many other factors to be taken into consideration and adjustments that would need to be made to the multiple. You should expect to consider multiple comparables and different operating and financial metrics to apply multiples against, but hopefully this illustration provides some concreteness to how an investor may establish an expected returns profile for your business. Ultimately, you must determine whether your company's circumstances justify the value you're pricing your company at today, the value you believe you can achieve by executing your business plan, and in turn, the returns you're presenting investors based on the slice of equity you're offering for their investment.

In the Pitch

To be clear, no investor is going to expect you to talk about IRR during your pitch. The point of this chapter is to show you how VC funds evaluate prospective investments and what is important to the economics between the general partner and its limited partners under their limited partnership agreement. Hopefully, in doing so, we've helped you understand why presenting an opportunity to beat the stock market or double their money in five years are unattractive pitches to VC funds.

Rather than IRR, in nearly all pitches investors will talk in terms of what multiple of their original investment they can expect to receive, but that's not because they're thinking about return on investment. It's because they consider so many prospective investments that they can do the fast math in their head to estimate the IRR you're offering based on a normal exit path from three to seven years. As an example, if an investment made on January 1, 2020, was worth 10X its value on January 1, 2027, the IRR would be ~47 percent.

25

Valuation Isn't Everything

IF YOU have ever seen a hot-seat reality investment show such as *Shark Tank* or *Dragons' Den*, you have likely witnessed a part where an investor and an entrepreneur negotiate some of the terms of the investment. Often this begins with the entrepreneur stating how much money they are seeking and the share of company ownership they are willing to offer in exchange. There might be a short back-and-forth over the company's valuation, but in almost all deals struck on television, the only point of negotiation with a lead investor is the valuation (and the corresponding implications for dilution). In the background, there are many more negotiated points.

Not to spoil the Hollywood magic, but even if an investor agrees to a deal on a TV show, they still need to go through a formal due diligence process. Plenty of deals struck on a TV show die on the vine once investors get a look under the hood and entrepreneurs consider the full set of terms an investor is offering. Perhaps some claims in the pitch affecting value were exaggerated, or it could be that other investment terms are disagreeable.

We understand why producers of these shows focus solely on valuation. It is far more entertaining to watch a high-stakes "who will blink first" debate over a single dollar figure the audience can wrap their heads around than cutting to a scene of lawyers emailing each other. A major misconception born from watching these negotiations is that investors are buying shares from the company with the same rights and privileges as those shares held by the company's other shareholders. One might assume the investor is offering to buy common shares in this emerging company. In reality, most sophisticated venture investors buying equity are not buying common equity.

The Problem with Common Equity

The basic rationale for holding equity is you will be entitled to share in the company's profits based on your ownership relative to other equity holders. In exchange for these potential profits, you and your fellow equity holders assume the risk that if the company falls apart, you will be the last group of people paid out from whatever value (if any) is left after its assets are sold and its debts are paid.

This simplified scenario assumes everyone holds the same type of equity—namely, common equity—with the same rights. While raising money by selling common shares is typical for larger, more established companies, this is almost never the case for early-stage companies. Why?

Imagine you and a friend are developing a cool new app showing real promise. You both decide your app has enough commercial potential to build a company around, so you plan and execute a capital raise and gather $2 million from a group of investors in exchange for 20 percent of the common equity of your company. (If 20 percent of your company's equity is worth $2 million, that means the other 80 percent is worth $8 million and the total post-money valuation is $10 million.)

Time passes and your app picks up traction, but it never grows beyond a small and passionate user base. A large tech company interested in your app and its user base soon offers to buy your company for $8 million, which you and your co-founder keenly accept. Remember, your investors invested based on the company being worth $10 million.

Since the investors have common equity of the same class as you and your co-founder, they have no special rights that would prioritize them. They simply take their relative share of the purchase price the buyer is paying for the shares. When dividing the $8 million among your common equity holders, the investors who first believed in you and invested the initial $2 million and received 20 percent will receive just $1.6 million (20 percent of $8 million). They bought high ($10 million) and sold low ($8 million).

Meanwhile, you and your co-founder divide the remaining $6.4 million among yourselves, making you both wealthy. In this scenario, your investors took a $400,000 loss to watch you both become millionaires!

Yes, in this scenario the investors who lost money accepted the risk that accompanies investing in your company at that valuation and on the terms agreed. Now you should see why sophisticated investors who will not tolerate such risk avoid acquiring common equity by making use of alternatives.

Alternatives to Common Equity

Investing in risky early-stage companies often involves alternative instruments that allow investors to own an interest in a business while providing significant protections against some of the potential downsides. You don't need to be an expert in all aspects of these alternative instruments, but you'll want some familiarity before taking meetings. If you receive an indication of interest to invest, it's very likely one of the following instruments will be the proposed investment mechanism. Being aware of these options can help your raise, so here are some brief descriptions of preferred shares and convertible instruments.

Preferred Shares

Preferred shares or preferred stock, sometimes colloquially referred to as "prefs" (rhymes with chefs), are a type of equity security used often when investing in emerging companies. Just like when a company issues common shares, when issuing preferred shares, the company's board sets a valuation and offers investors an opportunity to purchase equity—but this time, preferred equity. Unlike common equity, preferred equity comes with special features that give the holders additional rights, privileges, and protections beyond what the common equity has.

One of the special features often sought by venture investors is a liquidation preference. A liquidation preference gives an investor the right to be paid out first (i.e., before the common or other lower classes of preferred equity) under certain circumstances, such as when a company is sold or is winding up its operations and shutting down.

Investors seek liquidation preferences in young companies for downside protection if the company is liquidated or forced to sell at a valuation lower than when they invested. The liquidation preference feature lets the investor lower their risk profile on the downside, which makes the investment far more appealing.

For an illustrative example, let's return to our app developers who received $2 million from investors for a 20 percent stake of their company and later sold the entire company for

$8 million. Now, assume their investors had a basic liquidation preference giving them a priority right to either receive their investment back or receive their 20 percent share. In this scenario, the investors would opt to get their $2 million back, rather than receive 20 percent of the purchase price, as that would only be $1.6 million. Rather than lose hundreds of thousands of dollars, they would have at least broken even—not great, but better than a loss.

Alternatively, if the company performed superbly and sold for $50 million, those investors would pass on their right to receive their liquidation preference and would opt to receive their 20 percent interest, or $10 million. This feature effectively would have protected the new investors if things didn't go well, while allowing them to enjoy the upside if things went great.

Pay close attention to any liquidation preference in a term sheet! You might think an investor would have the right only to be paid out an equivalent amount to what they invested, but the terms of every preferred equity investment are unique. For example, an investor may have the right to get paid out on their initial investment *and* receive their respective percentage of whatever is left. It's also possible for an investor to aim for a liquidation preference equal to a multiple of their initial investment, such as 2x or 3x. Nodding your head and accepting whatever is presented, with the assumption that you are seeing "standard terms," may result in you inadvertently handing over more than is necessary or intended.

Liquidation preferences are commonplace in early-stage fundraising. Some of the largest public companies today had to accept them as they were raising capital in their early years. For example, prior to going public in 2021, Robinhood Markets investors had just under a $2.2 billion liquidation preference.

Liquidation preferences are just one of many special features that can be attached to preferred equity, and we will explore more of these later. In the interim, keep in mind that even though a company is setting a valuation when it issues preferred shares, the presence of these features means that not all the company's shareholders will necessarily share equally in the risks and rewards.

SAFEs and Convertible Debt

Sometimes investors recognize that an investment opportunity has exceptional potential but don't know how to set a valuation. For example, the ultimate product or service's unit economics could be hazy, the legal and regulatory environment is opaque, or the timelines for launch are murky. In these circumstances, it can be extremely difficult to establish a value the entrepreneur and investor can agree on.

Therefore, investors may look beyond equity for a security that allows them to invest without committing to a valuation. This approach can be particularly attractive for entrepreneurs who may find it impossible to set, defend, and support a valuation given what they have achieved so far, but are loath to accept what they might see as a punishingly low valuation.

One way this is done (often by angels) is by investing using a SAFE note. A SAFE (Simple Agreement for Future Equity) note is a security enabling the holder to convert the value of the SAFE note into shares of the issuing company when a defined future event occurs. This future event is usually the company completing a new financing round that sets a valuation, a so-called "priced round." This future event may also be the sale of the business or the liquidation or winding up of the business. The number of shares the SAFE note holder receives when this event occurs is based on the conversion mechanisms set out in the SAFE note. There are a couple ways these mechanisms work: via a discount or a valuation cap.

Discount

A conversion formula using a discount mechanism converts the SAFE note's value (principal plus any accrued interest, which is likely zero) into shares based on a discount to the price that the investors in the company's next fundraising pay for their shares.

Imagine that one year ago a company raised $1 million through a SAFE note with a 20 percent discount feature. Now the company is raising $3 million in an equity financing. It is selling shares to new investors for $1.00 per share and the pre-money valuation of the company forces the SAFE note's conversion.

In this scenario, the value of the SAFE note converts into equity at $0.80, which is a 20 percent discount to the price new investors are paying. Using the $1 million SAFE note example, and assuming no accrued interest, this means the SAFE note holders would receive 1.25 million shares for an investment of $1 million, while new investors would purchase 3 million shares for an investment of $3 million. Altogether, 4.25 million new shares are issued in the round. The 1.25 million share issuance for the conversion of the SAFE note is calculated by the SAFE note value divided by the result of applying the discount to the purchase price per share in the round. In other words, $1 million divided by the result of $1.00 multiplied by 80 percent equals 1.25 million shares.

If an investor invests at too high a valuation when the economic potential is extremely difficult to ascertain, they risk the company being forced to raise money at a much lower valuation when the value becomes clear. Alternatively, if they try and grind an entrepreneur down to an extremely low valuation, they risk the entrepreneur walking away from a deal. By using a discount feature in a SAFE note, investors can participate in emerging opportunities while mitigating the risk associated with prematurely setting a valuation, and getting upside through a pricing advantage in a later round.

Valuation Cap

A valuation cap, often shortened to just "cap," is a mechanism that gives investors the right to convert the value of their SAFE note into equity at the lower of the capped price, and the price in the company's next qualified round of financing. (This means they could get to pay a much lower price per share when their SAFE converts to equity.) While investors may be happy to own shares at a defined discount to your next priced round, they may also want to have the optionality to be rewarded for their early support if you become the next big thing. After all, from their perspective, their early investment helped you become the next big thing.

If holders of a pre-money SAFE note agreed to a cap of $10 million, and the company crushes expectations and raises money in its next round at a pre-money valuation of $40 million, then the SAFE note holders could convert into equity as if the company was raising money at a pre-money valuation of $10 million. To calculate the price per share the SAFE note holders pay for shares, divide the valuation cap by the round's pre-money valuation (i.e., $10 million divided by $40 million).

This means if the company is proclaiming to have a $40 million valuation when selling shares to new investors at a price of $1.00 per share, SAFE investors could convert their SAFE note as if they were buying at $0.25 per share ($10 million divided by $40 million multiplied by $1.00). That SAFE note with a $1 million principal investment and no accrued interest would convert into 4 million shares ($1 million divided by $0.25 per share).

It is not uncommon for a SAFE note to have both a discount and a cap, with the investor typically having the right to convert using whichever option yields the most shares. (Note that there is a difference between pre-money and post-money SAFE notes and how they convert, so make sure to clarify which type an investor is offering before proceeding.)

Convertible Debt

SAFE notes were first introduced in 2013 by Y Combinator, a famous Silicon Valley accelerator. Awareness of SAFE notes' functionality and acceptance among investors has continued to gain traction since. Prior to their introduction, investors who wanted some of the flexibility now offered by SAFE notes (picking up an early stake in a company without necessarily committing to a valuation) would use convertible debt. Convertible debt, just like a SAFE note, typically has a feature allowing the holder to convert their debt into equity based on a discount to the next priced equity round or a valuation cap. (The mechanics of a SAFE note are functionally derived from convertible debt.)

The use of convertible debt remains alive and well when investing in early-stage companies. One of the biggest reasons for its persistence is the protection it offers if things go sideways. If a company blows up before managing to raise more money, convertible debt holders have stronger legal mechanisms to be made whole from whatever value can be salvaged. For this reason, convertible debt tends to be more common when a company has more tangible assets that can be used as collateral, in contrast to SAFE notes, which are more common among asset-light tech companies in their early stages.

With that in mind, convertible debt has far more terms to negotiate than a SAFE note, including interest rates, debt maturity, events of default, and what assets it will be secured against. SAFE notes don't normally accumulate interest and when it comes to conversion—they do so only when certain events occur. A traditional convertible note, on the other hand, normally does pay interest (even if not in cash) and can usually be converted at the holder's option. This can make negotiations take longer and increase the associated legal costs. Therefore, many new tech companies and their investors tend to prefer the simplicity and speed of a SAFE note. You can imagine why an investor wouldn't want to bother incurring the additional cost and complexity of negotiating for convertible debt if the only things they can take should the company go belly up are a few laptops, office chairs, and lines of code.

Higher Is Not Necessarily Better

Obsessing over getting a "good" valuation is an easy way to miss the forest for the trees when negotiating. By no means should you give away something for less than its worth, but recognize that valuation is only one key factor among a broader negotiation involving other important matters.

Setting too high a valuation can be just as dangerous as going too low. You don't want to set yourself up for a down round (where your company's valuation is less than in a prior round) and the potential downsides that accompany it. If you are forced to raise money at a lower valuation, you may find you now need to manage the ire of your earlier investors. Focus on agreeing to a reasonable valuation and balancing it against the other terms relevant to the governance of the company.

There are investors who will look at a high-risk opportunity and sign up for common shares despite the risk involved. Not many, but they exist. Though they're not likely the kind capable of writing the biggest checks or adding the most other value. Raising money by selling common shares is entirely possible when a company is mature and its economics and equity returns are better understood, but you must get there first. You should expect to deal in the world of prefs and SAFE notes; don't assume a higher valuation is always better.

The Rule of 40 for Software Companies

If your company is a software as a service business, you'll want to be familiar with the Rule of 40 popularized in the public sphere by Brad Feld and Fred Wilson in 2015. Once your business reaches a certain level of sales maturity (e.g., ~$1 million in monthly recurring revenue), investors will likely use this rule to benchmark your company against other potential investments. The rule states that a software company's combined revenue growth rate and profit margin should be at least 40 percent for some defined period of interest (likely a year).

So, if your revenue growth rate is 60 percent, but your profit margin is 0 percent (for now), or your profit margin is negative 20 percent, but your revenue growth rate is 80 percent, you're still in good sorts. However, if your revenue growth rate is 15 percent and your profit margin is 20 percent (good metrics by any normal business standard, but aggregating to only 35 percent), that won't cut it. You likely won't garner much investor attention. The metric allows investors to get a sense of how your business can balance the trade-off between growth and profitability. If you're under 40 percent, investors may generally conclude that your company's growth and profits will not cover one another (or, put another way, the cost of growth exceeds the benefits).

The Rule of 40 can help frame your expectations for the valuation multiple investors may apply to your business. Meaning, the number they will multiply your sales by to determine your company's value. In late 2022, if applying the Rule of 40 to your company had yielded a result of 60 percent or more, it was possible to get a valuation reflecting 12x to 13x the sales. If you were in the 40 to 60 percent range, you would have been looking at around 7x to 9x the sales, and under 40 percent would have yielded something more like 2x to 3x the sales. The multiples vary based on market conditions, but you can see how valuation changes significantly as you go up or down the scale of the Rule of 40.

Case Study: Describing a SAFE Note Conversion

1. SAFE Note Issued

Venture Co. (the "company") issues a pre-money SAFE note for gross investment proceeds of $1 million.

The SAFE note will convert using a 20 percent discount or a $6 million valuation cap, whichever is better for the investor.

The company has 5 million common shares issued and outstanding prior to issuing the SAFE note.

2. Qualified Financing Causes Conversion

The SAFE note's conversion trigger is the completion of a Qualified Financing.

The SAFE note defines a "Qualified Financing" (or other similar term), which may be based on the occurrence of any equity issuance meeting a certain size threshold that sets a valuation for the company.

Say the company negotiates with a new equity investor to receive a $2 million investment based on an $8 million pre-money valuation (that results in a $10 million post-money valuation). This means the investor is taking a 20 percent interest in the company on a post-money basis. Based on the 5 million common shares outstanding before the investment, the $2 million investment would result in the issuance of 1.25 million shares (5 million divided by the result of 1 minus 0.2) for a price per share of $1.60 ($2 million divided by 1.25 million shares).

3. Discount or Cap Applied?

When a Qualified Financing occurs, the SAFE note will convert (in this case, applying either a share price discount or pricing based on a valuation cap).

Discount method. If the SAFE note converts under this scenario, the number of shares issued to the holder is calculated by reducing the share price using the discount rate (in this case, 20 percent). The $1.60 share price would be discounted by 20 percent ($0.32) to $1.28. Given a $1 million investment, 781,250 shares ($1 million divided by $1.28 per share) would be issued to the SAFE note holder.

Valuation cap method. If the SAFE note converts relying on a $6 million valuation cap, the number of shares the SAFE note's investment value converts into is determined by first dividing the valuation cap ($6 million) by the number of common shares issued and outstanding prior to the Qualified Financing. Based on the 5 million shares outstanding, the applicable price per share would be $1.20—a pre-money valuation of $6 million divided by 5 million shares. In this scenario, given a $1 million investment, 833,333 shares would be issued—$1 million divided by $1.20 per share.

Given that the SAFE note will convert based on what scenario is best for the investor, the valuation cap method would be applied because it would result in more shares (833,333 shares) being allocated to the investor as opposed to the discount approach that would net just 781,250 shares.

4. Post-Conversion Equity

After the Qualified Financing, Venture Co. would have 7,083,333 shares outstanding: 5 million belonging to the original shareholders, 1.25 million belonging to the new equity investors, and 833,333 belonging to the SAFE note holders. Keep in mind that new equity investors in your company will know the details of your existing SAFE notes before they invest. This means they will factor the dilution resulting from conversion into their valuation of the company. In this way, a large number of outstanding SAFE notes can lead to lower valuations in future priced rounds.

26

Accept Rejection with Grace

AFTER SPENDING days preparing for a meeting with a partner at a major VC fund, the day has finally arrived! The fund manager greets you and leads you to a boardroom where you and your team will make your pitch. Less than five minutes in, the manager picks up his phone and begins texting. Just a few moments later, his executive assistant walks in, tells him he has an urgent phone call, and he departs.

After patiently waiting thirty minutes, you walk out of the boardroom and ask his assistant if the partner needs to reschedule. The assistant tells you there is no need and the partner "saw all that they needed to see" and "will be in touch if he is interested." Your follow-up emails over the next two weeks are ignored, and you do not hear back from the fund again.

We understand why, after an experience like this, you may feel the need to tell off an investor. After all, they wrote you off without asking any follow-up questions or listening to your whole pitch—that you'd spent weeks preparing! To blow off steam, you draft a long email calling out the partner for his rudeness, telling him he has "no vision" and that, given how he treats founders, you "hope he goes broke."

Before pressing send, take a few deep breaths and delete the email.

Handling Rejection

Throughout your journey scrapping for funds, countless people will decline to invest. Many will not even reply to your pitch, no matter how many hours you spend researching and writing a carefully crafted email just for them. Much like in book publishing, screenwriting, and any other commercial activity involving the sale of any kind of product or service, there will be people who are simply disinterested, even if your idea has the potential to be exceptionally lucrative.

There are many reasons an investor may turn you down that are unrelated to the quality of your idea and business plan. Your idea may go beyond the scope of the investor's expertise, so they feel uncomfortable investing. You could be pitching a fund that is allowed to invest only in companies at a certain life cycle stage. They may invest only in companies that are generating revenue, so your pre-revenue business is too nascent for them. It is also possible you are pitching an investor pretending to have money even though their ex-spouse cleaned them out years ago, but they still take meetings with entrepreneurs because they like the attention. (It's rare, but it happens.)

Most funds and individual investors who turn you down won't give you the reason why. They do this because they do not want to turn their comments into a back-and-forth discussion where you try to win them over by convincing them their criticism is misplaced or that you can change. More practically, they do not have time to help you when they have nothing to gain and there are literally hundreds of other pitch decks waiting in their inbox. Time is money, and they don't have a reason to spend either on you at this point. It's not that they're mean. They're people. Most are good, some aren't. They're just doing their job and must spend their time wisely.

Regardless of why an investor chooses not to invest in your business, under absolutely no circumstance should you lash out at or insult them. This is especially true when it comes to social media posts. Even if you think they are in fact "short-sighted" or outright "incompetent," the small boost to your ego that flows from telling them off is not worth the consequences that may come from doing it. Moreover, you could be wrong. Regardless, it is straight-up unprofessional, and others will hear about it. By attacking them, you are doing more harm to your own reputation than you realize. Scorned investors may warn their own networks of co-investors about you, and none of them will be interested in meeting someone who behaves that way.

Remember that even if a prospective investor is not interested now, they might be later. A fund that turns you down because you don't have a finished product could be interested in investing in your next round after you have made more progress. If you lash out at them for not subscribing to your current round, you are burning a relationship with a potential future investor for purely emotional reasons. It's not personal time, it's business time.

Mental Health

Handling criticism and rejection from investors is important for raising money, but it is also critical for your own mental well-being.

Many entrepreneurs who are shown the door by credible investors, especially if it is done brusquely without any consideration, feel this rejection on a deeply personal level. If you pour your heart and soul into a company and prioritize it over every other opportunity and thing you could otherwise do with your time, it is very easy to subconsciously intertwine your own identity and sense of value with that company. So, when someone who you might consider an authority on your market outright rejects your idea, whether they heard your whole pitch or not, it can be deeply demoralizing.

It's important to acknowledge a few things. First, subject-matter experts and lead investors you speak to are not infallible. They have their own biases, and any who are honest with you and have been in business for any significant period would admit they have passed on deals where they could have made a fortune and instead parked cash in companies that bombed. This, of course, does not mean you should necessarily write off their opinions or rejections entirely. If you find yourself routinely unable to capture any interest, reflect and ask yourself hard questions about the opportunity you are presenting and whether you should consider making changes. Investment decisions are not easy ones. You have to help investors get to "yes."

The second thing to acknowledge is that your individual worth as a person is separate from the business you are pitching. Fantastically successful people have struggled with failure and perpetually tried to launch businesses that fizzled out completely before they realized success. Even if you cannot attract investor interest, it is a rejection of only one opportunity at one moment in time; it is not a rejection of you or what you are capable of in your life. Even the hardest venture experiences can be wonderful teachers that equip you with new skills and knowledge that will help you regardless of what you ultimately do.

27

Term Sheets and Series What?

YOU MAY encounter other entrepreneurs who have successfully raised money and tell you they "went on a roadshow" and just "closed on their Series B." Another might tell you they passed the hat around their friends and family to shore up enough money to complete their "seed round." If you don't meet these people, you'll surely read about them on LinkedIn or in the news.

It's fair to wonder whether these round titles mean anything. What's a seed round compared to a Series B?

Success Often Involves Multiple Funding Rounds

Many entrepreneurs who need to raise money for a new enterprise are mission driven. They're not looking for passive employment; they want to fulfill whatever purpose they are pursuing. If they envision their new technology being used by millions of people, or their branded product being carried by the world's top retailers, realizing that vision typically involves extraordinary amounts of money and other resources.

It is very uncommon for a business to raise these sizable amounts in a single fundraising round. Whether you have a fantastic idea is not the issue. As a practical matter, there are stages of development a business goes through. A business must get to checkpoints (milestones) that prove it is ready to move to the next stage and put the needed capital to work. Investors won't simply hand over tens of millions of dollars in high-risk capital to fund a "European expansion plan" without a working prototype. The future is uncertain and success requires more than money. It often requires steady, incremental progress over time, so capital is injected along the way. Fundraising is a continuous process for emerging companies. New rounds of capital are raised as the business proves its progress and achieves its milestones.

The frequency of these fundraising rounds varies based on the needs of the specific business and the entrepreneur's success in being able to raise previous rounds of capital. That said, emerging companies commonly aim to raise enough money in a round to sustain their operations for the next twelve to eighteen months. Companies generally don't want to raise an amount of money that will last less than twelve months, because the senior management team needs time to focus on building the business. They cannot constantly be hunting for money.

If a company raises enough money to last only a few months, and no significant milestones are met during that time, it could be very difficult to argue the company deserves a higher valuation at its next round. At least twelve months of runway is best. But when they are in survival mode, many companies will take what they can get when they need to cover expenses.

Round Terminology

As do other communities, the world of venture financing has its own jargon describing different phenomena. There are different terms describing different stages of fundraising. It's worth familiarizing yourself to avoid confusion when the term is thrown at you.

Before diving in, we should emphasize these are *not* terms with definitive formal legal or technical definitions. Rather, these are frequently used terms with generally agreed meanings. With that in mind, here are some guidelines for these frequently used terms.

Seed Rounds

When you hear the term **seed round**, picture a company in its earliest stages of development and financing. Seed money is generally raised from the entrepreneur's close personal network because the company could still be very much in its infancy, meaning only those with a high degree of trust in the founder may be willing to invest. That said, there are funds that invest in seed rounds. A company looking for seed funding is looking for support to take baby steps.

Participants in a seed round may include friends and family of the entrepreneur, which is why a company's earliest round is sometimes referred to as the **Friends and Family round** or an **F&F round.** Given the enormity of risk present at this stage, it is sometimes jokingly referred to as the "Friends, Family, and Fools round." Angel investors are also big players in seed rounds. They must be because many founders' friends and family don't necessarily have a few hundred thousand dollars in capital lying around they want to throw at a risky opportunity.

Various riffs on the seed round have emerged over the years. You could see people parse this definition depending on the situation. For example, an entrepreneur who raises a very small amount of capital just to tinker in their garage and work on a prototype may not want to call that raise a seed round and may instead call it **pre-seed** funding.

Alternatively, if a company has already gone through a seed round and is still finding its footing and needs more money, but isn't ready to approach a major fund, its founders may classify their next raise as a **Seed II round**. When a company has moved past these initial stages and feels they are ready for prime time, you will see them shift from the word "seed" to the word "series" when describing their fundraising rounds.

Series A and Beyond

The biggest inflection point in terminology occurs when a company has proved out its concept, (i.e., they have customers and are potentially generating revenue), understands its market and how to grow in it, and is ready to take things to the next level with the next round of financial backing.

Millions of dollars in funding to ramp up sales and hiring are likely required, so almost all founders will need to move beyond their personal networks. This is the stage when a company may first approach a venture capital fund or other deep-pocketed source of capital for their **Series A round**, if none was ever involved in any seed funding (though that's becoming less common).

After the Series A round, when a company requires more and more capital, the naming convention moves one letter down the alphabet with each successive round. In other words, the round following the Series A is the Series B, which is followed by the Series C, and then Series D, etc. This naming convention generally sticks if the company remains private, and falls out of use once a company goes public. Before they respectively went public, Lyft made it to Series I, Airbnb to Series G, and Shopify to Series C. It's also worth pointing out that a single "series" may have multiple closings. This is where some investors invest on one date and then a few weeks or months later some other investors come along and make their investment, but both sets of investors receive the same series of prefs (e.g., they both receive "Series C" preferred shares).

Tying these two discussions together, here is a table giving some *general* guidelines on each round, all of which change depending on market conditions. We must emphasize this: do not anchor yourself to these ranges. You may do better, you may do worse—and the market moves: what is normal for Series A one year may not be so the next. For Series A, there can be a lot of space between the average and the median investment amount.[8] It all depends on the strength of your company's prospects, your timing, and, of course, Lady Luck. The more a company can grow without raising money, the less dilution the founders will incur if they eventually do need to raise money.

Round Name	Investment Size	Valuation	Expected Dilution	General Objective
Pre-seed	>$0–$50K	>$0–$2M	10–15%	Prototype development
Seed	$200K–$5M	$2M–$20M	10–15%	Proof of concept
Series A	$1M–$30M	$10M–$50M	20–25%	Business model development, enhance user traction
Series B	$5M–$40M	$40M–$150M	20–25%	Accelerate growth
Series C	$30M–$100M	$100M–$1B	15–20%	Access new markets (scale), develop new products
Series D	>$100M	<$1B	10–15%	Pre-IPO/exit expansion

Here is some real-world data for the Shopify and Robinhood funding rounds based on their respective public filings and news releases:

INVESTMENT SIZE		
Round Name	**Shopify (NYSE: SHOP)**	**Robinhood (NASDAQ: HOOD)**
Seed	$250K	$3M
Series A	$7M	$13M
Series B	$15M	$50M
Series C	$100M	$110M
Series D	N/A (Public)	$363M
Series E	N/A (Public)	$373M
Series F	N/A (Public)	$600M
Series G	N/A (Public)	$660M
Series H	N/A (Public)	$3.4B
Total Equity Funding	**$122.25M**	**$5.6B**
Years from Seed to Last Round	~7 (Jan. 2007–Dec. 2013)	~7 (Dec. 2013–Jan. 2021)

Term Sheets

Now that the different rounds are clear, how should you expect these rounds to start off once an investor has shown their interest? You should expect to see a term sheet.

The term sheet will be an important document in an investment round, so you will want to wrap your head around its purpose and contents. Essentially, it is an initial expression of interest from an investor highlighting the terms of a proposed investment that would be captured in the investment agreement and governance documents (more on those later). The parties may capture these terms in one or several pages, depending on how detailed they wish to be. It sets out the initial understanding of the parties and a basis to work toward signing final contracts.

A bare-bones term sheet would typically include the amount of money being raised, the type of security being purchased (preferred equity, convertible debt, etc.), a clear or inferred valuation (if raising equity), and a prospective closing date. Term sheets will almost always include more detail than this; the level of detail depends on both the aims of the investor and the complexity of the security being purchased. Generally, term sheets outline terms related to economics, such as who gets paid when and how, how much, before whom else; and control rights, such as who has the power to appoint board members, what the board can approve, what must shareholders approve, and what level of authority will be delegated to officers.

Binding or Not?

Some elements of a term sheet may be binding whether you receive an investment or not, such as confidentiality and governing law provision. Other more important elements related to the key terms of the investment are almost always non-binding and can evolve over the course of the investment process. Of course, if they're agreed in a term sheet, there will need to be a good reason for them to shift, because anchoring bias and the spirit of good faith negotiations are powerful forces that resist change.

One reason terms may be renegotiated after signing a term sheet is if during due diligence a prospective investor discovers new information that influences their valuation of the business, or the amount of control they believe is required to guard their investment and promote the company's growth. Maybe they want to invest more, or maybe they found out the board had one more member than they thought, so they request another appointee.

In theory, an investor could offer favorable terms in a term sheet and then demand radical changes immediately before closing for no good reason, forcing you to either accept the new terms or start over with a new investor. This is not a practical strategy because the short-term win (if an entrepreneur acquiesces) is likely outweighed by the long-term consequences. Investors' reputations must be managed, and any investor who builds a reputation for this type of behavior will quickly find the best opportunities are no longer knocking on their door.

Drafting Responsibility

If term sheets are the initial expression of interest, you might expect investors to draft them. Like most things in business, it depends.

One of an entrepreneur's goals when fundraising should be to receive as many expressions of interest as possible. VC funds and large angels will typically draft their own term sheets, but sometimes companies receive interest from many small-check investors. These smaller investors often want the company to write the term sheet or wait on the sidelines for a "lead" investor (a VC or angel taking most of the equity in the round) to step in and set terms.

It is understandable that someone planning to write a $10,000 check for a $1 million round does not want to assume responsibility for drafting a term sheet (the legal fees alone may be close to half the value of the investment). Often this can cause companies to wander the abyss looking for a lead investor, particularly in their seed rounds. In these rounds, it can be best for the company to set terms rather than waiting for a lead investor to appear.

For your reference, here is an extremely simplified sample term sheet:

This sample term sheet is a learning aide only and is not to be used as part of an actual raise or a transaction of any nature. This example has been purposely simplified and generalized for this book and may not be useful for or applicable to the circumstances of any given company. You are urged to engage legal counsel to assist with the preparation, negotiation, and execution of any term sheet your company may wish to prepare.

Summary of Terms for Sale of Series A Preferred Stock	
Company/Issuer	[COMPANY NAME], a [JURISDICTION] [corporation/ limited liability company] (the "**Company**")
Investor(s)	Investment Company, Inc. ("**Lead Investor**") and other investors acceptable to the Company
Offering	Issuance of 5,000,000 shares of Series A Preferred Stock ("**Shares**") for a price of $1.00 per share
Dividend	5% annual noncumulative payable at the board's discretion.
Investment Amounts & Valuation	(i) $[__] from Lead Investor and (ii) $[__] from other investors (together, the "**Investment**") $[__] post-money value including an unallocated employee share option pool ("ESOP") representing 15% of the Company's equity capital on a full-diluted post-money basis.
Use of Proceeds	The Investment will be used exclusively to develop the Company's business operations.
Anti-Dilution	Broad-based weighted-average anti-dilution rights, subject to standard exceptions.

ESOP	Option grants under the ESOP will have four-year vesting periods with 25% on a one-year cliff and the balance vesting monthly over the following 36 months.
Liquidation Preference	Upon a merger, acquisition, equity or asset sale, or other similar transaction, liquidation, or dissolution, Shares shall receive the higher of (a) 1.0x the purchase price plus accrued and unpaid dividends and (b) the amount to be received if Shares are converted into common stock.
Conversion	Anytime at a holder's option, or automatically upon an IPO or approval by a majority of preferred stock, with an initial conversion ratio of 1:1.
Shareholder Rights & Transfer Restrictions	Standard voting approval and veto rights for an investment of this nature. Shares will have standard right of first refusal, tag-along rights, registration rights, preemptive rights, and information rights. A drag-along right will be exercisable by holders of at least 65% of the issued shares of common stock determined on an as-converted basis.
Board	Board size: 3. Lead Investor designates 1 director. [Founder] designates 1 director. Common stock majority, determined on an as-converted basis, designates 1 director.
Closing Date and Conditions	Closing will occur on or before [DATE].
Exclusivity	For [NUMBER] days the Company will not solicit or accept any offers for the acquisition of its equity (other than related to compensation).
Governing Law	This Summary of Terms is governed by the laws of [JURISDICTION].
Confidentiality	The contents of this Summary of Terms and its existence are strictly confidential.
Expenses	The Company shall pay all professional fees and expenses reasonably required to close the transaction (with a cap of $[__]).

Non-Binding	Except for each of the "Exclusivity," "Governing Law," "Confidentiality," "Expenses," and "Non-Binding" sections, this Summary of Terms does not constitute a legally binding obligation and there is no obligation to negotiate in good faith. This is not an offer to sell or a solicitation of any offer to buy securities in any jurisdiction where the offer or sale is not permitted.

DATE AND SIGNATURES

Summary of Terms dated ______________________________

Company Representative ______________________________

Lead Investor ______________________________

28

Don't Obsess Over Exits but Plan Ahead

BEFORE PITCHING your business, recognize that investors have varying time horizons for when they expect to have their investment (which has hopefully grown) returned.

Most early-stage investors understand that when building a business from the ground up, it may take several years to realize a cash return. In rare cases, early-stage investors can be overbearing and make excessive inquiries about when they can expect their money. Frankly, investors in the latter camp probably should not be investing in early-stage companies, and you probably do not want to take their money. (For example, if you are selling someone on a five-year vision and they want to have their money out in the next six months, that's not a match.)

Regardless of whether an investor's investment horizon is long or short, though, no investor wants their money trapped in a business with no way out. Concerns about being unable to retrieve one's investment within a certain time frame is not just a point of personal investment philosophy; it can be a legal requirement imposed on investors, including those with the capacity to write some of the largest checks.

VC Fund Commitment Periods and Harvesting Periods

If raising money from a VC fund, it is valuable to have an understanding of their basic mechanics. It helps you better understand their incentive structure and some of the questions they may ask and why they may insist upon certain investment terms—particularly regarding retrieving their money.

Venture capital funds can come in a few different forms, but the most common legal structure is a limited partnership. A limited partnership involves two distinct groups: the limited partners, or LPs, who provide the overwhelming majority of the money to the fund, and the general partners, or GPs, who manage the fund and oversee the investments. The limited partners might be private investment managers, university endowments, or plain old rich people, but their shared motivation is to gain exposure to early-stage opportunities that they may not have the time or expertise to vet and oversee themselves.

The terms of the relationship between the limited partners and the general partner(s) are governed by an extensive document called a limited partnership agreement. This agreement sets out what fees the limited partners must pay the general partner to manage their money, how profits from the fund will be divided, what kinds of companies the fund can and cannot invest in, and, most importantly for this chapter, when money needs to be returned to the limited partners.

The lifespan of any fund can vary, but venture capital funds commonly live for approximately eight to ten years. Companies can take several years to mature into standalone businesses from their first few investments, so aiming for a shorter time horizon can be challenging. Robinhood Markets, for example, took seven years following its Series A investment in 2014 before listing its shares on the Nasdaq stock exchange in 2021. A fund's life can also be extended past its original term under certain circumstances.

At the end of the fund's life, the investors' invested capital and profits must be distributed to them. Investors have obligations that must be met by certain times, which is why the timing of distributions is important to them.

Given investors place guardrails around the timing of their capital returns and the length of time it can take a young business to achieve a liquidity event, the life of a venture capital fund is generally thought of in two periods. The first period, known as the commitment period, runs for approximately the first half of the fund's life. This is when the fund is making new investments. The second period is known as the harvesting period. This is when the fund exits (or at least tries to exit) the investments it made during the commitment period. So, how do the funds exit their investments?

Liquidity Events (Exits)

For an investor to exit its position in a private company and realize value, what is known as a "liquidity event" must occur. A liquidity event is a corporate event that, under the company's governing documents, permits investors to readily convert their ownership into cash (or liquid securities of another company). The most desirable from a founder's perspective is when a company either goes public or is acquired by another company.

When a company "goes public," some of its shares are listed on a stock exchange. This allows members of the public to freely buy and sell the company's shares that are trading on the exchange. Assuming the company's shares attract enough secondary interest from the investing public, your investors will be able to sell their position to new shareholders over time. (This is why registration rights are so important. More on those later.) These are the companies you hear of that trade on the New York Stock Exchange, the NASDAQ, or the Toronto Stock Exchange.

Just because a company goes public does not mean an investor will have an easy time selling its shares. If a company goes public but cannot attract adequate investor interest, the shareholders could have an exceptionally hard time converting their position into liquid cash. This means going public is not always the best exit, even if some of the most successful and well-known exits have come from go-public transactions.

When companies don't go public, hopefully they succeed in the more common approach to achieving liquidity and are acquired by another company or buyer. When this happens, an acquiring company could pay for the target company's equity with cash, the acquirer's own shares, or a combination of both. If the acquiring company is offering cash, or if it is a large publicly traded company offering its shares, this can be an attractive liquidity event. If the buyer is offering shares and it is a private company (meaning its shares don't trade on a stock exchange) or even a small public company with a low trading volume, the ability of you and your investors to turn those shares into cash is less certain, so the exit opportunity will likely be less appealing.

Read the Fine Print

There is a very reasonable chance that your company will not be acquired or go public on a timeline that works for all investors' needs. Knowing that your company may not achieve a conventional liquidity event within their desired time horizon, these investors may demand certain terms so they can get their money out even if no other investors get theirs. They know that hoping is not an investment strategy.

The structure and variety of investment terms are broad, so we will focus on a simple example you could encounter while negotiating with a VC fund. The term enabling the VC fund's recovery of money is a redemption clause in the VC fund's favor, which, if exercised, requires the company to repurchase the investor's position (potentially at a premium if certain conditions are met).

A common mechanic of such a term is that after a certain period following the initial investment, say five years, the company must buy back the investor's equity if the business has not completed a liquidity event. The clause may require that if the company does not have the cash on hand to repurchase the investor's position, subject to any applicable statutory protections, it must raise other capital (if it can) to comply with the buyout requirement.

These redemption clauses vary tremendously in their specific terms and conditions. Some are rather modest, while others can be very restrictive. If you are faced with one, always make sure you clearly understand any terms (and their implications) related to any investor's ability to redeem their investment. The details matter.

Plan Ahead

When you are raising money, it is easy to be cynical if investors ask about an exit plan. Given the rate of technological change and the chaos involved in building a business, why would you possibly be expected to know when or by what means you will achieve a liquidity event?

While you do not need an exact plan for what company will buy your business or the date you will go public, recognize that your investors are looking for a path to having their cash returned. Not speaking to their needs or understanding the terms they might present will hurt your ability to raise money. Remember, they need only one reason to say no.

It's no problem if you want to run your company for the next twenty years, but be cognizant that your earliest investors will head for the exit long before then. Having an exit plan for yourself, not necessarily to share with others, will help bring clarity to your focus and growth path. There is a demonstrable benefit to having a line of sight on your end goal. While you shouldn't obsess over exits, we strongly recommend crafting a plan early on, even if it is subject to change. After all, the exit is one of the most important milestones in your company's life cycle. You don't need to know who is going to acquire you or exactly when you will go public, but it's good to understand whether your company could be valuable to an existing company.

DIFFERENT EXIT PATHS

Go Public	Sell the Company
Airbnb	Android (acquired by Google)
Dropbox	Figma (acquired by Adobe)
Facebook	Instagram (acquired by Facebook)
LinkedIn	Mobileye (acquired by Intel)
Snapchat	Postmates (acquired by Uber)
Pinterest	SkipTheDishes (acquired by Just Eat)
Shopify	Skype (acquired by eBay)
Twitter	WhatsApp (acquired by Facebook)
Uber	YouTube (acquired by Google)

29

Pay Attention to Closing

YOU MET with several investors over the past few weeks and received great feedback! Your most recent pitch went so well, the investor jumped at the chance to do a deal and asked you to send investment documents immediately!

"Wait," you think, "I'm supposed to send them paperwork? The last interested investor said they would send me paperwork. Also, when I raised money from my friends, they just sent me a check. We didn't have any paperwork! What is going on?"

The first externally funded capital raise can take entrepreneurs aback, given the formality of the documentation needed to close. It is easy to forget that raising money is an intensely regulated practice when you first pass the hat around to your close friends and family. As your business develops and you begin approaching professional investors who don't remember when you were in diapers, there will be more formalities for you to understand to ensure you translate investor interest into cash in the bank.

Closing Documents

If an investor likes you, signs a term sheet, and the due diligence process goes well, the company and the investors continue working toward "closing." Practically speaking, closing involves negotiating and signing legal documents (in parallel with due diligence), the investor depositing money with the company, and the company issuing the purchased securities to the investor.

Even for smaller deals, this process can take several weeks or months while the investors, the company, and their lawyers hammer out the nitty-gritty details of legal documents, complete due diligence, and take any other ancillary steps that may be required to close. While the exact set of closing documents required for each deal may vary, we broadly group the essentials into three buckets.

- **Investment agreements.** Under the investment agreement, the investor purchases, and the company sells, securities. This document sets out exactly what the investor is buying, how much they are paying, and the risks they're assuming in making their purchase (investment). You may see an investment agreement referred to as a share purchase agreement, note purchase agreement, SAFE purchase agreement, subscription agreement, and so on. It all depends on the nature of the entity receiving the investment, the type of securities being purchased, the entity's jurisdiction of formation, and the preferences of the drafting attorney.
- **Governance agreements.** Going forward, the company and the investors are in bed together, and something needs to govern that relationship (including any other investors that jump in the sack). Who must sign off on the budget or

authorize the purchase of large capital expenditures? Does the investor get a first shot at investing in future financing rounds? Who is going to have representatives on the board of directors? What if a major investor wants to sell their equity? Can they force anyone else to sell to equity on demand, or if they try to sell without including other equity holders, can those other equity holders tag along and participate in the sale? These points will be negotiated with your investors, and your governance agreements are the documents that will legislate those terms. You may have heard of a shareholder's agreement, an investor rights agreement, a right of first refusal (ROFR) and co-sale agreement, or a voting agreement. These are some of the documents you could encounter that we generally consider governance documents. Together, they operate as the constitution for how the company's relationship with its investors will be defined into the future.

- **Evidence of interest.** Investors want to receive something specifically identifying and evidencing their interest in the company after they've invested. Hollywood has likely well acquainted you with stock certificates—beautifully inscribed paper with elegant text certifying that the person named thereon owns a piece of a company whose name appears on the certificate. You're actually much better off with a copy of the register of stockholders (or schedule of members, if you have an LLC) than you are with a stock certificate. This is because your stock certificate just tells what you own, while the register will tell what you and everyone else owns. We must admit, though, there's a small sense of joy in holding a physical certificate printed on fancy paper. Physical share certificates still exist, but they have become less common as digital records take their place. Some investors may ask for a certificate as proof of their investment and ownership of their shares of stock, but it's less and less likely.

Involving experienced lawyers in the closing process is essential for drafting and negotiating investment agreements and governance agreements that work. Great lawyers will identify warning signs that could threaten your company far into the horizon. They'll also keep you out of trouble and everyone marching forward toward closing.

Funds Flow

Once investors have received all the documents, signed and delivered signatures, and the lawyers have verified that all steps are complete, then the cash flows.

When closing an investment that involves multiple investors, those investors will often send their money to a lawyer's escrow account, rather than directly to the company. In an escrow arrangement, the lawyer ensures that all conditions required for closing, such as signing all definitive documents and receiving money from every investor, have been satisfied before distributing cash to the company. Investors tend to prefer this arrangement because should the deal fall apart, they have assurance their money will be returned to them.

Some investors are happy to send money directly to a company's bank account before the fundraising round has closed. They fill out their paperwork, wire the funds, and assume everyone else will do the same in short order. This is more common with a company's earliest rounds when there is a high degree of existing trust between the investors and founders. If you find yourself in this situation, we recommend you *not* spend any of that money until the round is definitively closed and you've received confirmation from your lawyer. Experience will teach you that regardless of how far along a deal is, it can fall apart even when you think it's in the bag. If for some reason the round doesn't close and you've already spent the money, you will be left holding a liability with no money to return to that investor. This is an ugly spot to be in, so avoid it and the risk of being the subject of a lawsuit.

Finish the Play

You don't want to fumble when you're just about to score. If you developed an amazing business plan, assembled a great team, crafted a compelling pitch, and won over an investor, we do not want you to blow it in the final moments.

Demonstrating that you have no understanding, or appreciation, of the difficulty of closing a deal is a good way to weaken an investor's faith in you. You don't need to be lawyer, but you'll want to understand the events that lead to closing and who needs to take initiative and when. You'll want to be keyed into what's going on and responsive as needed, rather than sitting idly on the sidelines. If you have questions, ask them.

Path to Closing

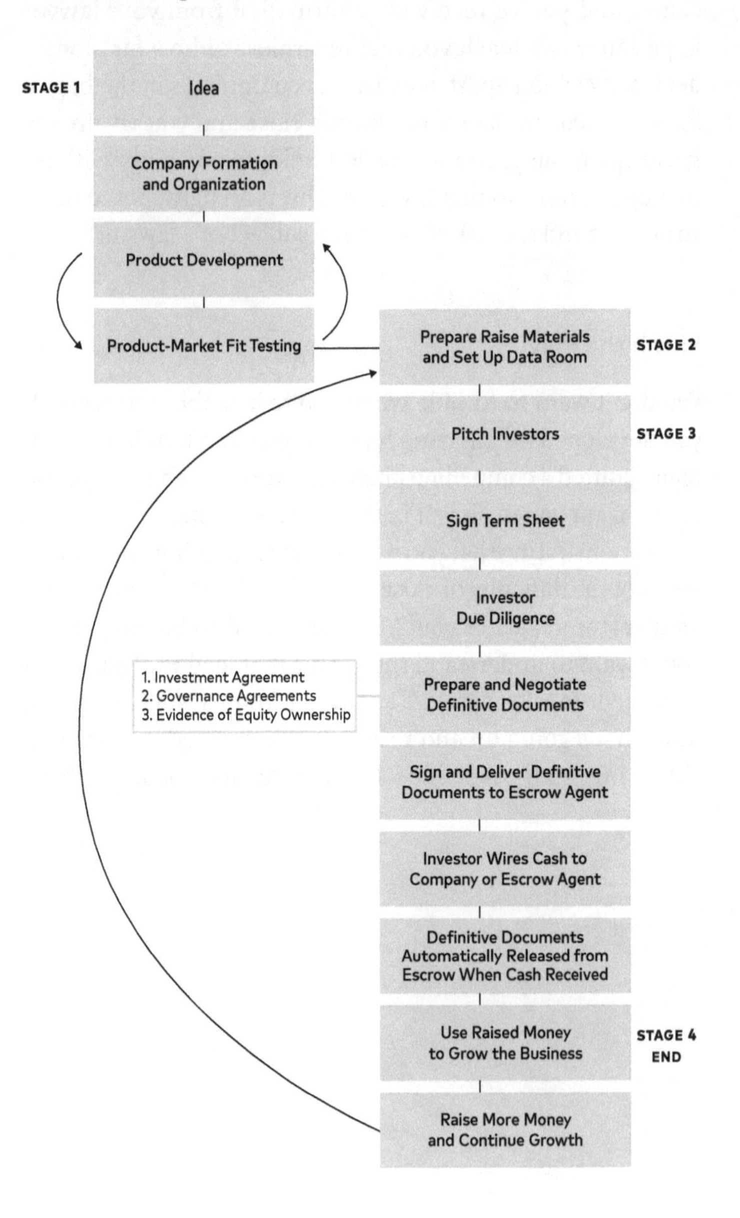

In stage three, the actual raise, we emphasized the importance of confidence, telling the truth, goal-setting, avoiding guarantees, setting reasonable salary expectations, understanding the returns investors expect, not focusing solely on valuation, and accepting rejection with grace. We also discussed crowdfunding, keeping focus through closing, and not obsessing over exits. Those discussions should better equip you to have conversations with investors, generate interest in your company, and secure an investment.

STAGE FOUR

AFTER THE RAISE

CONGRATULATIONS ARE in order! If you've made it this far as an entrepreneur, then all your preparation and hard work really paid off. Investors bought into your story and hitched a ride on the next leg of your journey. But they won't be silent, and they have certain expectations. The round is closed, but your journey has just begun.

Entrepreneurs have varying aspirations and objectives. Those with stars in their eyes hopefully recognize that their dreams will likely require raising money again in the future. Funding future growth with internally generated profits can be a real slog—or for some companies, outright impossible. This is why continuing growth likely depends on winning over new investors (and most likely convincing initial investors to send more cash your way) in the future.

There is more to closing the next round than simply advancing the company's technology or signing up new customers. Once a company has external investors, a critical legal and interpersonal dynamic between these investors and the company is formed. That dynamic must be understood and managed.

As your company grows and begins requiring larger checks from new investors, the level of scrutiny will increase considerably. Entrepreneurs must actively manage those relationships and establish internal processes to provide the requested informational updates, including information for presentation in subsequent rounds. It's likely you'll need to develop levels of internal sophistication that may not have been required in earlier fundraising rounds and to get comfortable with keeping investors in the loop.

After the raise, it's important to continue benchmarking against your competitors. You also need to engage in budget planning, navigate your governance structure effectively, and regularly communicate with your investors. You don't want to let issues with problematic shareholders fester, so you'll have to address them head-on, and you must give yourself lots of lead time when you know another raise will be needed.

Without further delay, let's review the work to do after the raise to avoid compromising the next one.

30

Benchmark Against Competitors

IF YOUR new business grew sales by 100 percent over the past year, you might feel pretty good about yourself. If you then found out your competitors all grew their sales by 500 percent and your product's total market grew by 300 percent, would you still feel so good?

Because the answer is clear, here are some follow-up questions: Is it sensible to focus on only your company's growth without making an active effort to understand how you compare to your competitors? If you don't know what your competitors are doing—what products they're selling, what services they're offering, or how they're fairing financially—how can you outperform them? Operating in isolation won't produce excellence. We talked in the ideation phase about understanding your industry, competitors, and other stakeholders; after the raise, many of these principles still hold and it may be time to implement a benchmarking process.

How can you compete for customers' dollars as you try to grow if you do not understand the players you're competing against? Winning those dollars will be much easier if you can effectively differentiate your company and your product in some way and ensure you're keeping pace with your competitors and others. Benchmarking helps achieve these goals.

As in sports, business competitors should compare themselves against one another qualitatively and quantitatively to better understand (1) what they can do well but their competitors can't, (2) what they can't do well but their competitors can, (3) what they can both do well, and (4) what they could both improve. You can view companies through many lenses when asking these questions, from the point of view of marketing, customer service, product quality, and so on. Answering these questions will help you focus on honing your strengths, improving your weaknesses, and exploiting your competitors' weaknesses. You'll become more competitive and, in turn, generate more long-term value.

You'll recall that the key pieces of information investors want to know are who else does what you're doing and how your offering is different. Essentially, they want you to see your product or service benchmarked against your competitors'. This helps investors understand where your company is in the marketplace, and will help them understand and value their potential investment. Benchmarking is critical at each stage: ideation, preparation, the raise, and after the raise. But it's not uncommon for companies to avoid the exercise. Reasons companies don't benchmark may include:

- Not wanting to spend time looking for data.
- Not knowing where to get data.
- Thinking benchmarking isn't useful.

Benchmarking is too important to strategy formulation and achieving and maintaining competitiveness to disregard.

Benchmarking should be a distinct and focused exercise your management team undertakes as part of its strategic planning process. Without benchmarking, how will you know how long you retain customers compared to the industry average, or how your prices fit in your market? These insights do not come from thin air.

Understand Your Industry Position

Benchmarking can provide a major wake-up call and give you actionable insights into how your company can strengthen and refine its strategy for success. Honestly assessing your company's weaknesses and opportunities can open your eyes to necessary adjustments. You can use this benchmarking data to develop targets for your company's key performance metrics against industry figures, and to measure your performance against those targets over time. This will ensure you can access important insights into whether changes you've made (or decided not to make) have had the desired effect. Modern markets are so competitive, you simply can't afford not to have this information.

Industry comparisons don't need to be quantitative or financial in nature to have value. It is important to understand how your company differs from others qualitatively, too. For example, it is helpful to know the level of brand recognition your company has (i.e., how many people are familiar with your brand compared to competitors'), or how customers' experiences with your product compare to your competitors and why. Benchmarking analyses of a qualitative and quantitative nature are critical to understanding your industry position and where your competitors may be outperforming (or underperforming) you.

The Benchmarking Process

Select Appropriate Metrics to Benchmark

You can benchmark almost anything, so make sure to benchmark metrics and data points that offer strategic value for your company. For example, you may want to arrange a market research effort to determine how customers view comparable products' price-performance differences against yours.

Store the Data

Generally, and not just for benchmarking purposes, you should store all the data you collect and use in business analytics in a usable and accessible manner. Whether you are compiling a database of time series financial data or tracking customer feedback, you'll need an organized process for storing, accessing, updating, processing, and analyzing qualitative and quantitative data so that benchmarking exercises can be automated wherever possible and made more efficient with each successive iteration. This way more time can be allocated to interpreting the results of the analysis, which is the real value of benchmarking. Also, you'll want to ensure all your team members are using the same process. In other words, don't have one person using Microsoft Access and another, OpenOffice Base.

Use Appropriate Comparables

Select a set of companies reasonably comparable to yours, such as your competitors. Then try to locate datasets describing your industry (or your competitors) in your target markets. If you run a technology company working on a data management tool, don't benchmark against a pharmaceutical company working on a cure for dementia. Only when you benchmark against others competing in the same space will you derive the most valuable insights. These direct comparisons will enable you to see how your company stacks up against others in various ways.

Tell the Data's Story

Extracting useful narratives from data is an art and a science, especially when aiming to identify representative narratives. Compelling visuals are a helpful way to explain to others whatever stories you find in the data. Graphics, charts, and graphs will help people absorb your message quickly.

Finding Data

Before you can analyze anything, you must gather the data you need. This can be difficult, particularly if you are looking for data on private companies. Searching for existing data is time consuming. You'll spend time looking for free sources and may cave in and pay data providers like PitchBook or KingsCrowd. So, once you find the right data sources, bookmark them immediately. If the data doesn't exist, then you may need to pay a research firm to gather it. Unfortunately, this can be expensive. The data you need is probably out there, but you must spend the time looking for and organizing it.

In the resource pages at the back of this book, we include some examples of data sources to consider. Some require payment or membership. In some cases, it could be worth it. These sources will have a lot of information that is irrelevant to your company. Often you must dig to find the golden nuggets.

Hopefully it's clear benchmarking can be a valuable part of your go-forward research regarding your competition and integral in identifying ways to improve your business. If you don't benchmark yourself against competitors, you will lack key information that can help you improve your ability to compete for customers' dollars.

31

Budget to Support Planning and Accountability

FOUNDERS CAN view drafting an annual budget as an annoyance, something done purely to satisfy a bureaucratic investor's checklist. Some believe their "market is so hot any budget will be outdated by the time it's written," so there is no point. Other times one may hear, "Things could change so quickly for the business that preparing an annual budget is a waste of time. What if we need to do a product pivot in three months?"

Regardless of the justification, anyone with this attitude to budgeting is completely missing the point of the exercise. Your budget will change over time. It doesn't need to line up perfectly with your original business plan. There will be unexpected inflows and outflows.

At the highest level, budgeting is done to align the various functions (sales, operations, etc.) and address competing priorities in a business. Once a budget is prepared, anyone in the company can look and see where resources are being used and better understand how the rest of the company interacts with their department—maybe they'll have some good ideas on how to be more efficient.

Hopefully they don't become sidetracked by some petty power game. Unfortunately, the budgeting process can cause departmental rifts. Your best chance of avoiding this is clear and up-front communication of priorities and decision-making rationales.

A budget is valuable because it provides a baseline of the costs you will incur and the revenues (if any) you expect to generate for the relevant period on your path to achieving your company's objectives. Without this baseline, you may quickly find yourself adrift and experiencing wholly avoidable financial crises. Under no circumstances do you want to become so financially disorganized that you need to call up your parents to bail you out so you can make payroll. (It happens.)

Without an up-to-date budget, how will you know if a large rent deposit or other payment is coming due and you need to set aside cash? If you don't check your budget regularly, you could forget about these obligations and inadvertently leave yourself without the needed cash on the due date. You obviously don't want that to happen.

A budget is a tool to help track whether your company is using its resources efficiently and performing as expected. It shows investors where and when money is expected to come from and what and when it will be spent on.

The most value you'll derive from this tool comes from monitoring it. At the end of a budget period, if you compare your "actual" spending, revenues, and losses to your initial forecasted numbers, you will see differences and be able to refine and revise your assumptions about your resource management and operational profile in your go-forward budgets.

If you see pronounced differences between your forecasts and your actuals and find yourself asking, "How the heck did that happen?" then it's time to put on your analytics hat. As part of that analysis, you're looking to understand how your performance deviations connect to your operations and strategy, so that you can begin acting to close the gap. Once you're doing this, you're using your budget properly. Even if you performed much better than expected and stayed right in line with your budget, it's still a worthy exercise to understand the roots of your strengths. While budgeting is a time-consuming process, revising, refining, and reprojecting your budget will help you understand that it is a valuable exercise.

What's in a Budget

Operating budgets are much simpler than you may think. You do it for your personal life; it's the same thing. Assign money inflows and expenses to categories and then net them out to figure out how much money you're making or losing as part of your operation.

Generally, in descending order, the categories you'll see in a budget spreadsheet are revenues (broken into driving categories such as volume and price per unit), variable costs, and fixed costs. Contribution margin is the difference between revenues and variable costs. Other items include depreciation, interest, and taxes. Budgets tracking these items monthly are common, but depending on the circumstances, you can design them for any frequency you wish. The rest is about accurately and consistently grouping expenses, recordkeeping, and software to prepare financial statements. Whether you do that in-house or by contract is another matter to consider.

ACCOUNTS	JAN	FEB	MAR	APR	MAY
Revenue	**$5,000**	—	—	—	—
Volume					
Product 1	100 units	—	—	—	—
Price					
Price 1	$50.00	—	—		—
Variable Costs	**$210***	—	—	—	—
Raw Materials	$2 per unit	—	—	—	—
Utilities	$0.10 per unit	—	—	—	—
VC 3	—	—	—	—	—
Fixed Costs	**$500**				
Rent	$500	—	—	—	—
FC 2	—	—	—	—	—
Development/ Capital Spending	**$1,500**	—	—	—	—
Net Cash	**$2,790****	—	—	—	—

* Variable Costs = ($2 × 50 units) + ($0.10 × 50 units

** Net Cash = $5,000 - $210 - $500 - $1,500

Budgeting for a Nascent Business

Budgets for early-stage companies, especially at the pre-seed and seed stages, are not traditional budgets. One way their cash flow profiles are very distinct from those of established companies is that an early-stage company is likely spending more cash than it is collecting every month.

The net amount of cash leaving the door each month is commonly referred to as the burn rate. Investors focus on a company's burn rate because they want to know how long it can survive before needing additional funding. For example, your burn rate might start at $40,000 per month, but as you need to scale production of your product, it might ramp up to $100,000 per month.

Investors know that the initial use of proceeds you proposed in your first pitch could change. They understand that every day you will be working just to survive, but they will still want to see the expected financial implications of decisions. You'll want to develop a general understanding of budgeting and get some basic financial knowledge, because you'll need it to make sound decisions taking into account financial matters. The budgeting process will help you think about costs in terms of variable and fixed, and to understand your company's revenue profile.

Critically, investors will want to see that you're learning how to budget funds for reinvestment in your business to generate a high return on investment. They are looking for disciplined and thoughtful budgeting that focuses resources on nurturing high-value activities. Capital discipline reflected through the budgeting process will be a keen area of focus for investors, so make sure it is one for you, too. For example, don't shy away from investing in products and features customers are positively and profitably responding to, while dumping more money into products and features you believe can work in the long run but customers have yet to eagerly adopt.

Budgeting Is Forever

Budgeting will never end. Get the right tools and systems in place to track your expenses, revenues, and other resources used. With that information you'll be able to access usable data to estimate how well you're sticking to your budget. As a simple example: you should have a chart of accounts to guide how you're categorizing specific variable and fixed costs your business incurs.

These account descriptions should be detailed enough for useful analysis and mutual exclusivity, but general enough for practicality. Anyone reviewing your financials or responsible for bookkeeping must be able to understand the makeup and purpose of the named accounts and confirm they are consistently populated with appropriate accounting items. For example, insurance costs should not be grouped with office supplies. You would have two separate line items. One for insurance, one for office supplies.

For your budgeting and expense tracking systems to be scalable, you must use appropriate accounting software and have written practices and policies in place so new team members can be smoothly integrated and responsibilities can be transitioned. If you haven't automated the entry and categorization of business activities that hit the financial statements, then someone somewhere is wasting a lot of time on manual entries. Use technology to efficiently track spending and log accounting entries.

So, what software should you use? QuickBooks is perfectly serviceable to start. If you're surveying options, don't get stuck in analysis paralysis.

Gathering Input

If you solicit input from the appropriate people, the insights will be more valuable. If you're a 100-person organization, you don't need (or want) to get budget input from every person, so you need to be selective. If there are only eight people working at your company, you probably want to hear from everyone. Part of leadership is ensuring decisions are based on a healthy foundation of information, including the views of others in your company.

Budget beyond Cash

Excellent budgets address more than financial targets and cash management. They analyze the management of other resources, too. This other analysis is not primarily financial, but has implications for the business's financial situation. To fully assess your company's performance, you need to look beyond financial metrics to other factors that drive the financials.

A more fulsome budget may lay out various perspectives of where the company should be, including financial (revenue, gross margin, etc.), customer (satisfaction scores, lifetime value, etc.), efficiency (operating leverage, inventory management, etc.), and growth (employee retention rate, process scalability measures, etc.). Building a budget with these dimensions helps you develop an understanding of your company's resource needs. It can also help reveal any disconnect between management's view of the business's needs and the actual needs (this becomes clear in the actual vs. planned budget comparisons). Using this information should improve managerial focus and help you find less expensive ways to operate, which will help you make money.

32

Governance Matters

EARLIER WE described the buckets of documents involved in commercial prenups (aka, investment agreements, governance agreements, and evidence of interest). It's time to dig deeper into the contents, because their terms are crucial to how the business is managed. Being flippant about the rights and privileges of investors could lead an entrepreneur into an ugly legal battle or, in extreme cases, even cost them control of the company.

When making major corporate decisions, you'll want to consult these agreements. You don't want to sink energy into an initiative and realize at the last moment that you need an approval or a waiver you can't get. Does anyone want to be about to close a major bespoke licensing deal, which has taken many hours from many people, without noting that their major investor has a veto right over licensing agreements outside the ordinary course of business, and that they don't have proper authority to sign? No matter the outcome, they'd sustain significant reputational damage with all parties involved if they had to delay signing for the investor's review and approval.

These summaries are brief descriptions of some key provisions of the governance agreements you will see often in venture deals. We're offering a high-level overview of these concepts for your familiarity, not a detailed textbook of every mechanic, bell and whistle, and negotiating consideration. That book will be long, dry, and kept on a corporate lawyer's bookshelf.

These are not easy concepts to wrap your head around, especially without context. This chapter may take a couple reads. When thinking about these concepts, it might be helpful to envision a company with one majority shareholder and some minority shareholders, say, two 10 percent minority shareholders and one 15 percent minority shareholder. This will help you think about how different shareholders may want protection in certain scenarios.

What if the company issues more equity? Do you want to maintain your ownership percentage? That's what preemptive rights are for.

Let's say the majority holder wants to sell the company to a buyer, but the other shareholders don't want to sell to that buyer. The majority holder can exercise its drag-along right to force the minority holders to sell.

What if one minority holder wants to sell their shares to an investor the other shareholders are unfamiliar with, and none are keen to welcome any others into the fold? Then a right of first refusal (ROFR) will sure come in handy.

What if the majority holder is planning to sell only its equity (rather than the whole company), but one of the minority holders wants to realize some liquidity too and does not want to stay as invested with that majority holder's interest winding down? Thankfully, this minority holder that had been left in the cold can rely on its tag-along (or co-sale) rights to ensure it gets a slice of the action.

Finally, no one wants to fund a company but have no assurance their shares will ever be listed on a stock exchange.

Without that listing, shares' liquidity potential is lower. That's why equity holders want registration rights with their equity.

Here goes.

Preemptive Rights

Investors want preemptive rights to maintain their relative slice of the pie as it grows. Preemptive rights allow the investor to buy a portion of any additional shares or equity securities issued by the company equivalent to its existing ownership share.

This keeps their ownership share in the company constant. In other words, if an investor owned 15 percent of your company and you went off to raise a new round, an investor with preemptive rights could buy shares in that new round sufficient to maintain their 15 percent interest post-financing. You can see how this right is only useful if you have the cash to act. If an investor has the capacity to use it, it is an effective means of protecting against dilution.

Preemptive rights are not absolute. They are often time-limited, so investors who have them must elect to exercise them in a limited window (say twenty to thirty business days) following notice of the new round.

Certain issuances of equity are normally exempt from preemptive rights. For example, issuances where the shares issued are being used as consideration to purchase another company do not permit exercise of a preemptive right—you can't short-change the sellers on the shares they're expecting to receive! Issuing shares as payment in a merger or acquisition and issuing shares to raise capital are very different corporate activities, so it makes sense for the preemptive right to apply differently in each scenario.

Transferring Shares

Restrictions on Transfer and Rights at Exit

The equity securities of companies that VCs invest in are illiquid (i.e., not easy to sell). Even if an investor can find a buyer, the company may not want that buyer to own those shares. What if the buyer is affiliated with a competitor and making the purchase for nefarious reasons? Stranger things have happened. Clearly, a company needs to be able to control who owns its shares, but owners still need some ability to transfer their equity. A balance must be struck. You could, perhaps, require board approval for a transfer, but with certain restrictions on who may be a transferee, and then give certain permissions to transfer to a limited set of people (family members, family trusts, affiliated entities, etc.) without board approval.

In a moment, we'll discuss drags and tags (co-sale rights) and ROFRs. Without general restrictions on transferring shares, none of these rights would mean much! If people could freely trade their securities in a company, it would be very difficult to maintain control of governance.

Generally, transfer restrictions are designed so security holders cannot transfer their securities to anyone but a select group of folks normally defined as "permitted transferees." Even then, if a permitted transferee won't sign a paper subjecting themselves to the terms of the company's governance documents, the transfer probably won't happen. Private companies working to grow want tight control over ownership. This is because shareholders get to elect directors, who can hire and fire officers and completely change the power dynamics of a company. Obviously, that can significantly alter its direction, strategy, and operations.

Drags and Tags

A drag-along right allows one or more of a company's security holders to force all the other security holders to sell their securities to a particular buyer. Think of it as a forced sale right. Drag rights can be very robust and powerful, to the point where a single investor can force a company sale, regardless of what other owners want. They can even require the others to sign documents to get the deal done.

Thinking back to the scenario where a majority holder wants to sell but the minority holders aren't interested, the drag comes in very handy. Usually, buyers want the whole business and don't want to be constrained by, or deal with, the holdouts, so the drag ensures a small group of holdouts can't torpedo the deal.

Tag-along (or co-sale) rights are adored by minority investors because they protect against a single investor selling its shares and leaving the others out in the cold. In a situation where a majority holder is selling its shares to a third party, and a minority holder doesn't want to be involved in the company without that majority holder, the tag allows that minority holder to sell some of its securities as part of the majority holder's sale. Tags ensure investors can sell their shares and realize some value concurrently with folks (like founders and major investors) who may have more control of the business and whose stakes may be more attractive to buyers on a standalone basis.

How do tag-along rights work? The shareholder exercising their tag-along right gets to sell a portion of the number of shares being sold to the buyer, equal to the tag-along right holder's proportionate ownership of the company's shares. Say someone is buying 40 percent of the shares in a company, and you own 10 percent of that company. Normally, a tag would give you the right to sell 4 percent of the company's shares (i.e., 10 percent of the 40 percent of the company's shares being sold).

Redemption Rights

An investor's redemption right allows it to, at its option, force a company to repurchase the company's securities owned by the investor (at a specified price). We mentioned that investors' redemption rights can come up, and you should be aware of them in case an investor asks. The applicable purchase price (or method of determining it) at exercise of a redemption is negotiable when you're putting together the investment and governance agreements, not after they're signed, so do it up front.

Rights of First Refusal

A ROFR (pronounced "row fur") is exactly what it sounds like. It's a first bite at the apple. If a shareholder wants to sell their shares to a third party, the ROFR forces them to first offer to sell those securities to the company or the company's other shareholders on substantially the same terms that the third party is offering.

The company or the investors will have a set period to accept the offer. If they don't agree to buy the shares within that period, then the shareholder can sell its shares to the third party.

Astute readers may notice that tags and ROFRS have a structural relationship. If a controlling shareholder wants to sell to a third party, the ROFR is triggered, but if neither the company nor any other shareholder decides (or has the means) to exercise its ROFR, the shareholders can then use their tag to sell some of their shares as part of the sale to the third party and realize some return.

Voting Rights, Protective Provisions, and Director Appointment Rights

Shares (or LLC units) can come with a variety of built-in protections giving investors control or significant influence over a company's decisions. Different classes and series may have varying veto and board appointment rights. In many cases, an investor will have veto power over key decisions, such as changes to the authorized capital (the type and number of shares or other equity units a company can issue), setting annual budgets, whether to engage in mergers and acquisitions transactions (M&A) or a related-party transaction (where there may be a conflict of interest), and whether to issue debt.

In every raise, the specific rights are negotiated, so there can be some variance from deal to deal. However, unless a business is performing so well that the founder has all the leverage (which is extremely rare), founders should mentally prepare to cede significant amounts of decision-making authority to others. It's only fair. They are, after all, providing the financial means to accelerate the company's growth. It's extremely common for investors to get rights to appoint a specified number of directors to the board, so expect director appointment rights to come up.

Registration Rights

Registration rights are massively complicated and often occupy pages and pages of text. You will never want to read them—not even lawyers want to—but you should be aware of them.

Registration rights are all about achieving liquidity. Investors want these to ensure they get the benefit of public market liquidity premiums in connection with that snazzy IPO you're dreaming of so they, too, can sail off into the sunset with buckets of cash.

An asset is obviously more valuable with a bigger pool of potential buyers. The incremental value increase in the shares due to how much easier it becomes to sell them when they're listed on a stock exchange is known as a "liquidity premium."

Registration rights give shareholders the right to tell a company to register its restricted shares (i.e., shares that can only be sold to a limited set of people under securities laws) with the securities regulator, so those restricted securities can be freely sold to the public at a price that will capture the liquidity premium.

At the highest level, there are two categories of registration rights: there are "demand" registration rights and "piggyback" registration rights. The latter is obviously the standout star in name, but it is a weaker right in practice.

Demand Registration Rights

Demand registration rights don't come into play until after a company has its blockbuster IPO and the confetti settles. After that, investors with these rights can demand, at certain times (usually a couple times a year and following a sufficient gap after the IPO), that some of the company's restricted securities owned by early investors and subject to registration rights be registered for public sales (so investors can cash in via sales on the stock exchange).

You may wonder why this right is needed after an IPO. It is because usually only a fraction of a company's outstanding equity is sold to the public in an IPO, while a swath of securities are left behind in restricted securities purgatory but are considered "registrable" because they are subject to registration rights.

Piggyback Registration Rights

While less powerful than demand registration rights from an investor's perspective, piggyback registration rights allow investors to include their registrable securities or piggyback, usually on a pro rata basis, on any registration initiated by the company or another investor.

There Is More to the Story

Corporate lawyers may be aghast by the scant descriptions we have provided, but the point of this book is not to detail the economic and legal minutiae of these admittedly complicated rights. It is to make you aware of them and their general purpose so that you know what to look for and think about, and what to ask your lawyer, when investors put term sheets in front of you. If you need to read this chapter a few times, that's fine!

33

Communicate with Your Investors

YOU ARE an entrepreneur with an innovative idea, a fantastic team, and money in the bank from a successful raise. You are primed to disrupt your industry's short-sighted competitors and capture their customers. You know you will be stretched unbelievably thin managing your company's wild growth, so you figure that sending routine updates to your shareholders will only slow you down. You further reason that they'd prefer you focus on growth rather than waste time giving them information you're already on top of.

In almost all cases, though, this is not the way to go. Open communication will help you establish more trust and give you the most runway to get help solving the issues you're facing. Still, there are many reasons why entrepreneurs do not update their shareholders. Some do not think it is necessary, some do not see the value in sharing an update, and some are plainly disinterested.

The common thread among these explanations is, these founders do not believe their shareholders can help address any issue the company is facing other than by handing over money. Unfortunately, it is a big mistake to treat your shareholders like they have nothing to offer besides the cash they have already invested.

Shareholders Can Be Valuable Resources

Remember, your investors have already bought into your company and story. If they were not sold, they would not have invested. Now that your success and theirs are aligned, they, more than anyone besides you and perhaps your parents, want you to succeed.

As a founder, you must help your investors help you succeed. You do that by regularly communicating with them. Your updates to shareholders should not be just a summary of the latest sales figures or product launches. They should include calls for advice or action as needed. Whether trying to find new customers, a new hire to fill a critical role, or even new investors, your shareholders can potentially help with all these things if you let them know what you need.

Want your shareholders to bring in some sales leads? Tell them who a potential customer should call or email, what information that customer should have ready, what type of client would be an ideal fit for your situation, and where potential customers can learn more about your business. Don't send your shareholders just your mission statement about transforming an industry and expect that's all they need to give potential customers. Help them help you.

When done right, consistent investor communication can create a highly motivated auxiliary sales force. Investors have their own broad networks they see at weddings, reunions, and other parties. They meet people (who probably also have money) and talk about what is new in their lives, including investments. Even if one of your shareholders does not know anyone who can help you at a certain point in time, it does not mean that will always be true.

Compromising the Next Round

It should come as no surprise that when you go to raise your next round, one of the first investor groups you will reach out to are your current shareholders. After all, they understand your business, have already invested, and (if you have been successful) may be keen to double down.

If you have been providing regular updates to your shareholders before you go to speak to them about a new financing round, they are more likely to listen. Even if things have not gone according to the plan in your first pitch (they never do), the fact that you have been regularly updating them about developments demonstrates competence, organization, and respect for the business and its capital. If you have not been communicating and your first call is to tell them you need more money, it's going to be a rough call.

In many cases, entrepreneurs do not reach out to their shareholders until they are so desperate for cash, the business is on the precipice of collapse. Entrepreneurs may do this because they are scared of disappointing their shareholders or being chewed out, but waiting until the last minute will only make it worse. If you have never heard a phone call from an entrepreneur telling an investor, who they have not spoken to in eons, that they need money immediately or the business will fail, let us assure you that you do not want to.

Not all shareholders are going to fire off a note telling you that you should be providing them with more updates—many will just expect it of you. Irritating your shareholders through a lack of communication can be a slow shift toward contention, and the consequences may not be obvious until you are in a bind. The consequence of not communicating is that your pissed-off shareholders become less likely to subscribe to your next round, and also less willing to bring their network of fellow investors into your world.

Communicate, Communicate, Communicate

We've been hammering the point that it's important to communicate with your investors, but you might reasonably be asking, "How often should I communicate?" Updating your investors at least once a quarter is an absolute must. That said, three months can feel like an eternity in the fast-moving venture world, so more frequent updates (perhaps once a month) should be considered. They should not be a daily or weekly thing—investors do, after all, want your primary attention to be on growing the business they sank their money into. Of course, these are guidelines, and you should talk to your investors to set up a reporting procedure that works for your circumstances.

Note that if you have already received an investment, you will want to review the terms regarding shareholder updates. Your governance documents might include a section called "Information Rights," which specifically requires you to provide updates at a certain frequency and with certain details. While less common with early venture opportunities, these rights can even require you to produce audited annual financial statements, which are neither cheap nor quick to produce, and the consequences of not complying can be serious.

There is no universal rule for how often you should update your investors. Use your judgment and behave in a way that would keep a person trusting you. When in doubt, reach out.

Blown Raise Story: Waiting for Good News

A group of friends, hardcore fitness fans who all worked for the same apparel company, decided to launch a new brand of athletic wear. They had a fantastic mix of expertise, including design, production, digital marketing, and more. They built a plan and budget for what they hoped would be the next great fitness brand. They raised a sizable sum from their extended personal network off the strengths of their team and story, and got to building.

During the first few months, the CEO kept her shareholders in the loop about all the great developments transpiring. From getting office space, to onboarding new hires, to booking meetings with top retail outlets, she kept her investors informed. While she didn't have regular updates scheduled, she would fire off frequent emails containing whatever great news came across her desk.

After six months of operations, the company started running into considerable roadblocks. Production costs far exceeded the budget, a few new hires were poached by competitors, and the founders received a letter from their former employer's legal department asserting they were in violation of their non-competition agreements. The CEO was worried all this bad news would spook the shareholders, so she planned to share her next update once the company had some good news to share in hopes this would soften the blow.

Unfortunately, bad news kept piling up, while good news remained elusive. New investors kept turning them down, their manufacturers said they would need to wait months longer than expected, and they started to run out of money. After six months of radio silence, the CEO finally reached out to her investors and told them that they were facing serious challenges, and without a capital injection in the next month, they would be forced to close.

The investors were understandably apoplectic. They asked the CEO how this desperation for cash was possible for the company after all the great news. They also wondered why this was the first time they were hearing of the many challenges. The CEO tried to explain how things would change if they just got a little bit more money, but the investors wouldn't hear it. None of them agreed to help the company in its hour of need, and it folded.

34

Address Problematic Shareholders Immediately

SHAREHOLDER PROBLEMS are often, at their core, people problems. The longer people problems fester, the more likely they will morph into legal problems, which can scare investors or derail your company. Nip them in the bud quickly and decisively. Then return your focus and energy to value creation. These issues are much easier to handle if you mitigated the risks by implementing an appropriate governance structure and adapting that structure as needed as the company grows. Perhaps you did, but if you've completed a fundraising round, the investors likely forced you to in any case.

At the early stages, likely only key executives (and maybe a few angels) will have shares, so those are the "people" involved. They may have had divergent views on many critical business points that required resolution before you were ready to move forward with commercializing your innovation and seeking VC funding.

Views can diverge once more. Some may want to sell what you've already built and bail. Others may be committed to taking the company public. Still others may think the product needs more time in development before it's ready for the next phase of growth. A few may be gung-ho to start increasing focus on scaling. Reconciling these positions when everyone's full buy-in is critical to success is no small task, and it can make or break the company's success.

We've hit hard on the point that misallocating equity can create many headaches when you're trying to raise money. You're past that, so thankfully it wasn't an issue for you, but it bears repeating that a black hole on your cap table filled by some shareholder who stopped caring about the business will haunt any entrepreneur hoping to raise funds. For the sake of repetition: you mustn't hand out equity lightly. Any equity you distribute must be properly designed to align that person's and the company's interests, so the individual is incentivized to drive the company's growth. Otherwise, you will have shareholder (people) problems. Post-raise, you'll need the consent of others on the board, so this is less likely to be an issue.

Still, if someone involved with the operation and holding 10 percent of the company stops contributing to the cause and is delaying progress, it is a serious problem. Especially if you can't get a replacement because the necessary incentive equity is tied up with this person who turned out to be all hat and no cattle. This is why it's very important that you have a cohesive and incentivized management team and appropriate vesting conditions attached to equity grants.

How would you get a person to forego their equity if they believe there is value in the business as is (and yet refuse to do any more work), especially if you have no legal mechanism to recapture their equity? In another case, what if this person has a totally different view of the growth path than you do? They will then be significantly disincentivized by your chosen path. They may think it leads to certain failure, so they think their equity is worth nothing and soon leave for something else. Hopefully, you threw vesting or repurchase rights on their equity, and hopefully any voting power is contingent on their continued engagement with the company. If not, sparks may fly.

Internal Bickering Is Scary and Wasteful

Time focused on resolving internal squabbles is a drag on growing the business, which no one wants. Who wants to put money into an entity incapable of going full throttle because of fundamental disagreements among shareholder executives? Or in an entity where it's uncertain whether the key folks involved have truly bought into and aligned on the vision? No one, that's who.

Depending how central the issue is to the company's value, and how open the grumbly shareholder is to resolution, you may need to tee up a replacement with an equivalent skill set. You'll want your advisors' (financial and legal) thoughts on your planned next steps. Be sure to discuss how those next steps serve your strategy for achieving your desired outcome in this shareholder conflict. It could be that you want better alignment of that shareholder's incentives with the company's, or you might want them gone no matter the cost. Whatever it is, we don't necessarily recommend getting your lawyer openly involved in communications with the other shareholder, or even telling them you're talking to your lawyer (both of those are probably very unhelpful steps). Instead, have your lawyer work with you in the background from the time you start trying to resolve the issue at a business level. And run your written correspondence by them *before* you send it to the problem person.

Be Decisive

The best way to address internal shareholder issues is through constructive discussion. In the most contentious cases, though, you want to be able to rely on your governance agreements to oust someone if necessary.

Following a raise with a sophisticated investor, you'll have these documents in place, so use the mechanisms available in them. If for some reason your governance documents don't have the necessary provisions to address the situation, then start putting together a plan to minimize damage. Unfortunately, this will be another distraction. It will be more complicated, too, because you must persuade the problematic shareholder to sign these new documents. In either case, once the path is charted, you must be decisive and committed to your chosen strategy. We've seen business progress be derailed for nearly a year while leadership worked to resolve shareholder squabbles.

Act Quickly

Do not let rifts between shareholders build. Address them head-on. Do not assume that just because you are not aware of any issues, there are none. Do a little research. Talk to your key people to understand where their heads are at. Make sure people are comfortable talking to you, and develop their trust. This trust is very important because internal bickering can delay raises and cause opportunities to pass by. You can stay in front of potential issues by having strong relationships with key shareholders. The window for success is often fleeting, so you don't want to waste time on value-destroying infighting.

35

Future Raises May Take More or Less Time

AFTER CLOSING a major round, there can be a real and vibrant sense of optimism and purpose. It is likely your team is growing. New products are hopefully flying off the shelves, and your company's social media accounts should be buzzing and accumulating followers in a way you only wish your personal ones would. Though profitability may remain elusive, your business is demonstrating healthy momentum. You're confident there is a path to profitability and continued growth, if you don't run out of money before you get there.

Few companies with grand aspirations will raise enough money in a single round to carry them through to the end game (or to a point where they are profitable enough to self-finance through the end game). You'll likely need to endure one or more additional capital raises in the future. For example, Lyft made it to Series I before its IPO.

There will come a time when, upon inspecting your company's bank balance or your burn rate analysis (which you dutifully keep current), you will realize that more money needs to be raised soon to continue operations and make payroll.

No Two Rounds Are the Same

You may remember that your first round among friends and family took only a couple of weeks to close, and maybe your Series A took just three weeks, so you figure you have loads of time. Unfortunately, one raise can be very different from another. No matter how many you go through, it's best to allow time for unforeseen difficulties. Some rounds close fast, some take months. Best to be conservative in your planning.

A myriad of factors can influence how long a round takes to close. Investors may want terms changed halfway through the process when, during due diligence, they discover something untoward. One investor may drop out or cut their commitment, so another needs to be found. Maybe your first raise took place at a time when markets were frothy and people were throwing cash around with less scrutiny—but times change. Maybe when you go to market now, you're faced with colder shoulders and more scrupulous financiers due to more reserved market conditions. It's difficult to foresee all the factors that could influence your business's particular circumstances and what the capital markets will be doing when you need to tap them, so we'll say it again: be conservative in your planning.

Maybe in your next round, you'll raise only from existing investors with whom you've maintained a respectful working relationship and appropriate level of trust. In that case, you will probably have a quicker turnaround time than if you're onboarding someone new who must be persuaded to buy into your vision and run a fresh due diligence process.

The point is, don't assume your next round will happen on the same timeline as the last one. Plan for further raises well in advance (at least three to six months).

It Pays to Be Prepared

You've raised money before, so investors will want to know what you did with it and whether you managed it efficiently. They'll want to see that you've met your milestones and stayed on the path you projected, or understand why you deviated. Achieving corporate milestones is a clear priority for any good CEO. It will be harder to raise money in subsequent rounds if you haven't achieved your projected milestones using the funds you previously raised.

If you haven't achieved those milestones, at least provide a good reason why you didn't and explain why you pivoted to other areas of focus that represented a wise and value-accretive use of capital. Investors need to see that you have capital allocation skills and that your decisions grow the value of the business.

Being ready to discuss these matters and defend your decisions is an essential part of continuing to build on existing levels of trust with prior investors and establishing it with new ones as you pursue subsequent rounds. You'll need time to prepare crisp and rational answers. With everything you'll have going on, you'll need to give yourself plenty of lead time.

Refresh and update your presentation materials, prepare new materials as needed, and start talking to your existing investors and advisors. Remember, investors always want to see strong forward momentum. Avoidable cash flow problems due to poor planning can bring businesses to a grinding halt and destroy progress already made. In any case, such problems can be enough to kill your raise and, with it, your business, so plan ahead and don't create a cash crunch.

Stage four was all about discussing the time after the raise. We emphasized how important it is to continue benchmarking against your competitors and that you must actively engage in budgeting. You'll have to become accustomed to navigating your new governance structure effectively when making decisions, and communicate with shareholders regularly while addressing problematic ones swiftly. To make sure you don't let a good thing falter, you must give yourself plenty of lead time when you see the next raise on the horizon.

If you do all these things after raising money, you'll be on a path to keeping your business capitalized with the necessary financial resources to succeed. This will allow you to focus on what really matters: developing and selling a great product that delivers tremendous value to your customers. If you can do that and navigate the fundraising process, we have no doubt you'll be successful.

Epilogue

WE HAVE endeavored to equip you with knowledge to make fundraising for your business less stressful by discussing a broad base of topics. This knowledge will make you aware of and prepared for key issues you will face.

We built this work upon four pillars, or concepts, which support a diligent approach to raising money for a new venture.

First, establish trust with investors and earn their confidence. Do this through your actions *and* your words. Actions (like being on time and prepared) are your most effective means of communicating to investors that they are taking a reasonable risk by investing in your business and your team.

Second, organizations need organization. From meetings to key documents, to data rooms and beyond, successfully raising money and running a sound operation requires an organized approach, so you can keep track of your milestone progress and underlying operations, and demonstrate competence to investors (thereby building trust) throughout the process.

Third, without a persuasive pitch clarifying the value proposition of your product or service and its commercial potential, it will be difficult to receive a check.

Fourth, while you will shoulder much of the fundraising burden yourself, to be successful, you'll need to rely on subject-matter experts and build a competent team.

We hope this knowledge serves you well! We wish you nothing but success on your next big raise.

Notes

1. "What Does a General Partner Do?," AngelList, learn.angellist.com/articles/general-partner; "VC: GC Commit," Venture Patterns, venturepatterns.com/blog/vc/vc-gp-commit.
2. Mark Suster, "Your Product Needs to be 10x Better Than the Competition to Win: Here's Why," Both Sides of the Table, bothsidesofthetable.com/your-product-needs-to-be-10x-better-than-the-competition-to-win-here-s-why-6168bab60de7.
3. Tom Eisenmann, "Why Start-ups Fail," *Harvard Business Review*, May–June 2021, hbr.org/2021/05/why-start-ups-fail.
4. Noah Parsons, "What Is a Business Model?: Business Models Explained," Bplans, 2017, updated 2021, articles.bplans.com/what-is-a-business-model-business-models-explained.
5. *United States v. Elizabeth A. Holmes, et al.*, 18-CR-00258-EJD, United States District Court, Northern District of California, San Jose Division (October 13, 2020).
6. Kelly Hoey, "Why Your Startup Needs an Advisory Board," *Inc.*, April 13, 2017, inc.com/kelly-hoey/why-your-startup-needs-an-advisory-board; Jake Mendel, "Building Your Startup Advisory Board," Silicon Valley Bank, svb.com/startup-insights/startup-strategy/building-startup-advisory-board.
7. Artturi Tarjanne, "Why VC's Seek 10x Returns," *Activist VC Blog*, Nexit Ventures, January 12, 2018, nexitventures.com/blog/vcs-seek-10x-returns.
8. Jason D. Rowley, "The Distribution of Series A Deal Size in the US," Crunchbase News, February 10, 2020, news.crunchbase.com/venture/the-distribution-of-series-a-deal-size-in-the-us.

Resources

THROUGHOUT THIS book, you will have noticed references to the resource pages. Here it is! This section contains further resources that expand upon topics we address in our writing that may help you raise capital. Most of these resources are universally applicable, but a few, such as those relating to taxes and grant programs, apply only to certain jurisdictions.

Other Great Capital-Raising Books

Exit Path: How to Win the Startup End Game, by Touraj Parang

Raising Angel & Venture Capital Finance: An Entrepreneur's Guide to Securing Venture Finance, by Dr. Tom McKaskill

The Startup Game: Inside the Partnership Between Venture Capitalists and Entrepreneurs, by William H. Draper III

Venture Deals: Be Smarter Than Your Lawyer and Venture Capitalist, by Brad Feld and Jason Mendelson

Intellectual Property Books and Resources

Guide to Intellectual Property: What It Is, How to Protect It, How to Exploit It, by Stephen Johnson

Kohler Legal: Intellectual Property Starter Guide for Entrepreneurs & Small Businesses (kohler.legal/business-law-articles/intellectual-property-starter-guide)

Patents, Copyrights, & Trademarks for Dummies, by Henri Charmasson and John Buchaca

World Intellectual Property Organization: Patent Cooperation Treaty Member States Map (wipo.int/pct/en/pct_contracting_states.html)

Understanding Your Competition Resources

"How to Track Your Competitors," *PitchBook Blog* (pitchbook.com/blog/how-to-track-your-competitors)

GlobalSpex: The Top 8 Competitor Research Resource List and Tools (globalspex.com/what-to-research-about-your-competitors)

"Sizing Up the Competition: How to Conduct Competitive Research," by Jamie Johnson (uschamber.com/co/start/strategy/how-to-conduct-competitive-research)

Key Performance Indicators Resources

BSC Designer: Full Guide to KPIs: Examples and Templates (bscdesigner.com/kpis-guide.htm)

"Startup Killer: The Cost of Customer Acquisition," by David Skok (forentrepreneurs.com/startup-killer)

"What Is a KPI? A Complete Guide to Key Performance Indicators," by Dale Pearson (geckoboard.com/blog/what-is-a-key-p erformance-indicator-kpi)

Pitch Deck Resources

"23 Best Startup Pitch Deck Examples: Famous in Tech (For 2022)," by Tomas Laurinavicius (business.tutsplus.com/articles/startup-pitch-deck-examples--cms-33037)

Failory: "50 Pitch Decks from Well-Known Series A Startups" (failory.com/pitch-deck/series-a)

"35 Best Pitch Decks from Real-Life Startups [With Templates]," by Orana Velarde (visme.co/blog/best-pitch-decks)

CB Insights: "The Early Pitch Decks of 29 Startups before They Became Billion-Dollar Companies" (cbinsights.com/research/billion-dollar-startup-pitch-decks)

Investment Document Samples & Resources

MaRS: Sample Funding Templates (for Ontario Investors and Entrepreneurs) (learn.marsdd.com/article/sample-funding-templates-for-ontario-investors-and-entrepreneurs)

National Angel Capital Organization (Canada) (nacocanada.com)

Y Combinator: Safe Financing Documents (ycombinator.com/documents)

Links to Business Analysis Frameworks and Examples

"A PEST Analysis Template for Any Industry or Business," by Kiesha Frue (pestleanalysis.com/pest-analysis-template)

"Analyzing Starbucks' Value Chain," by Prableen Bajpai (investopedia.com/articles/investing/103114/starbucks-example-value-chain-model.asp)

Creately: SWOT Graph Templates (creately.com/diagram-community/popular/t/swot)

"How Competitive Forces Shape Strategy," by Michael E. Porter (hbr.org/1979/03/how-competitive-forces-shape-strategy)

Links to Select Grant Programs

NRC IRAP Funding to Hire Young Graduates (Canada) (nrc.canada.ca/en/support-technology-innovation/nrc-irap-funding-hire-young-graduates)

Small Business Innovation Research (U.S.) (sbir.gov)

U.S. Federal Grants—Grants.gov (grants.gov)

Pitch Competitions

Collision's PITCH (collisionconf.com/startups/pitch)

MIT $100K Entrepreneurship Competition (mit100k.org)

TechCrunch's Startup Battlefield

Financial Modeling Resources

Kruze Consulting: Startup Financial Models: Numbers That Explain Your Startup's Potential (kruzeconsulting.com/five_tips_for_startup_financial_health/startup_financial_models)

"The Founder's Guide to Financial Modeling," by Dave Lishego (PDF) (cmu.edu/swartz-center-for-entrepreneurship/assets/Olympus percent20pdfs/founders-guide-to-financial-modeling-dave-lishego)

"The Ultimate Guide to Financial Modeling for Startups," by Wout Bobbink (ey.com/en_nl/finance-navigator/the-ultimate-guide-to-financial-modeling-for-startups)

Links to Select Tax Advantages/Disadvantages for Entrepreneurs

U.S.

FreshBooks Blog: Your Complete Guide to 2023 U.S. Small Business Tax Credits (freshbooks.com/blog/8-tax-credits-every-small-business-owner-should-know-about)

U.S. Department of the Treasury: Small Business Tax Credit Programs (home.treasury.gov/policy-issues/coronavirus/assistance-for-small-businesses/small-business-tax-credit-programs)

CANADA

Mentor Works (mentorworks.ca/startup-resources)

Scientific Research and Experimental Development (SR&ED) Tax Incentives (canada.ca/en/revenue-agency/services/scientific-research-experimental-development-tax-incentive-program.html)

Market Research Data Sources

Data.gov (U.S. government) (data.gov)

Electronic Data Gathering, Analysis and Retrieval System (U.S.) (sec.gov/edgar)

Financial Times (ft.com)

IBIS*World* (ibisworld.com)

KingsCrowd (kingscrowd.com)

National Bureau of Economic Research (U.S.) (nber.org)

OpenCorporates (opencorporates.com)

Pew Research (pewresearch.org)

PitchBook (pitchbook.com)

Software & Information Industry Association (siia.net)

System for Electronic Document Analysis and Retrieval (Canada) (sedar.com)

Technology & Services Industry Association (tsia.com)

U.S. Department of Commerce, Bureau of Economic Analysis (bea.gov)

World Bank: Doing Business Database (databank.worldbank.org/source/doing-business)

Index

Note: Page references in italics refer to figures or tables

About the Authors

Michael Miller, MBA

Michael is a Toronto-based financial professional specializing in valuation, transaction structuring, and equity analysis. Michael previously worked for two venture capital funds and currently specializes in M&A at a Canadian media conglomerate. Michael has been quoted and featured as a financial expert across several platforms and publications, including BNN Bloomberg, *Business Insider*, MarketWatch, *Vice*, and the *Financial Post*.

Michael is the co-author of *"High" Profits from Accounting for Cannabis Plant Industry*, the world's first accounting business case about the cannabis industry, which was published by the University of Cambridge's Judge Business School. Michael also guest-lectures on financial subjects at several colleges, including the University of Cambridge (UK), York University (Canada), Toronto Metropolitan University, and George Brown College. Michael has an MBA from the Schulich School of Business (2014) and an undergraduate degree in history and East Asian studies from the University of Toronto (2008).

Alexander Baker, JD, MBA, CFA, MA (Econ)

Alexander is a corporate attorney in Dallas at an international U.S.-based law firm where he maintains an M&A, private equity and venture capital practice, working on a wide array of transactional and governance matters for public and private companies, and private equity and venture capital funds.

Before moving to Texas from Silicon Valley in late 2021, Alexander practiced at another international U.S.-based law firm, in Palo Alto, and previously held a similar role at a Canada-based law firm in Calgary, Alberta.

Alexander completed his JD/MBA (2016) in Toronto at Osgoode Hall Law School and the Schulich School of Business. He holds a master's degree in economics from Wilfrid Laurier University (2010) and an undergraduate degree in economics from McMaster University (2009). Alexander earned the Chartered Financial Analyst (CFA) designation in 2018.

WANT MORE?

When we set out to write *The Big Raise*, we wanted to create a resource to help entrepreneurs who need venture capital raise it successfully. Nothing will help us achieve that goal more than our readers, such as you, rating and reviewing this book. Whether you engage with us on social media or rate and review our work on our website or your preferred online retailer's, these engagements will help us reach a broader audience.

If you have your own story of a successful or unsuccessful raise that you believe can help others succeed, we would love for you to post your story so we can help even more entrepreneurs understand what to do and what not to do.

Find and tag us on social media and visit our website!

𝕏 Michael: @Porters6thForce
Alexander: @HowNotToRaiseMoney

in Michael: linkedin.com/in/michaelacmiller
Alexander: linkedin.com/in/alexander-baker-1346065b

thebigraise.net

Hire Us

Like shooting a film, a challenge with writing any book is leaving lots of pieces on the cutting room floor. We have a bevy of experience with raising money, and many of the best lessons are offered in person. Each of us—Alexander and Michael—is available to speak at conferences, corporate events, and educational workshops, and offer our years of experience to expand on the contents of *The Big Raise*. Reach out to us for rates and availability.

Bulk Purchases

If you are at an institution—like a business school, accelerator, incubator, co-working space, fund, bank, or other body that believes its stakeholders could benefit from our work—we provide special bulk order rates.

Contact orders@pagetwo.com for details.

Made in United States
Troutdale, OR
03/09/2024